Beyond the Incident

Practical Tools, Legal Causation and Applied Workplace Investigation Practice

DESAI LINK

Beyond the Incident
Desai Link

Digital Discovery Limited
New Zealand
2025

ISBN: 978-0-473-73917-1

This book is typeset and published by the author.
Cover design by Nir Schnapp. Photo by @DreamsToLenses
First Edition: June 2025

Disclaimer

The information contained in this book is provided for general informational and educational purposes only. It is not intended as legal advice, nor should it be interpreted as a substitute for professional consultation with qualified legal, health and safety, or regulatory experts.

While every effort has been made to ensure the accuracy of the content, laws and standards can vary between jurisdictions and change over time. The author and publisher accept no responsibility for any loss or liability incurred as a result of actions taken or not taken based on the information in this book.

Readers are encouraged to seek appropriate professional advice relevant to their specific circumstances.

In memory of my father, Steven Thomas Link —

Your integrity, work ethic, and quiet strength shaped the way I show up in the world. This book carries your influence throughout.

Table of Contents

Foreword

Desai Link (Des) is a Certified OHS Professional and an admitted lawyer to the Western Australian Supreme Court Bar, bringing a unique blend of legal expertise, risk management, and hands-on safety leadership to workplace health and safety. A native of Perth, Australia, Des has spent his career operating in high-risk industries such as construction, transport, oil and gas, leading and conducting large-scale and complex workplace investigations. His expert analysis has helped organisations strengthen safety outcomes, enhance compliance, and implement robust risk management frameworks.

I first met Des back in 2013 on Chevron's Gorgon Project-one of the largest natural gas infrastructure projects in the world, estimated to cost $55 billion USD to build. During its six-year construction, the project had a workforce of 8,500 people on site at any given time, building colossal infrastructure in one of the most inhospitable and remote locations on Earth. Barrow Island is a place where temperatures regularly soar beyond 45°C, and the Fly-In, Fly-Out (FIFO) lifestyle demanded a level of resilience that few could sustain. It was here, under these extreme conditions, that I first saw Des in action.

We connected quickly, driven by a shared dedication to safety, risk management, and the pursuit of excellence in OHS. As I joined the HSEQ team, I had the opportunity to watch Des work-and what stood out was his dedication, methodical approach, and relentless pursuit of improvement.

Des excelled at navigating stringent client safety standards, staying ahead of legislative changes, and delivering high-impact training and operator verifications. But his real strength lay in investigations. He had a clinical yet deeply human approach, balancing technical precision with genuine curiosity. His talent for identifying causes-often uncovering critical factors that others missed—was remarkable. His findings were always defendable, built on meticulous evidence gathering, detailed analysis, and open, honest witness interviews. He understood something that many fail to recognise: a strong witness statement is built on trust. Des had an uncanny knack for establishing trust instantly, approaching every situation unbiased, prepared, and focused letting the facts reveal the truth.

Des has since gone on to act as an expert witness, advise on critical safety failures, and develop hazard mitigation strategies that have shaped industry standards. His innovative approach to cutting safety bureaucracy while improving real-world risk management has earned him widespread industry recognition.

Des is a respected speaker, lecturer, and thought leader. He lectures on workplace safety law at Auckland University of Technology, his insights have been featured at leading industry conferences, and he is a host of the "Circus of Safety" podcast, where he and his co-hosts explore contemporary safety challenges.

Now based in New Zealand, Des holds a senior OHS position within a major construction organisation, working to improve safety standards in one of the country's highest-risk industries. He has seamlessly integrated into New Zealand's OHS risk management landscape, earning respect from construction industry safety groups and worker safety advocates alike.

From the blistering heat of Barrow Island to the ever-evolving challenges of high-risk industries, I've watched Des navigate some of the toughest environments with precision, integrity, and an unwavering commitment to getting safety right. His ability to cut through the noise, find the real issues, and drive meaningful change is something I've always admired.

Now, through this book, others get the chance to see what I've seen firsthand-an approach to safety that is clear, pragmatic, and deeply rooted in experience.

Des doesn't just talk about safety; he lives it. And that's what makes this book worth reading.

– Jared Kane (MPP OHS)

February 2025

Preface

"...understanding how accidents occur is fundamental to establishing interventions to prevent their occurrence"[1]

I decided to write this book because I saw significant gaps in the way workplace safety investigations were taught and undertaken. I noticed that causation models promoted in the work health and safety industry often overlook centuries of causation analysis developed in legal case law. I also observed investigation methodologies being taught that disregard investigation ethics and the legal methods of obtaining and evaluating oral evidence. By applying these legal methods and tools from my own experience, I believe investigations can be more effective and efficient.

I believe that investigating, as a skill, is one that requires constant learning and practice. It would be misleading to assume that completing a single, two-day investigation course is sufficient grounding for a workplace incident investigator. Similarly, gaining experience in workplace incident investigations alone is insufficient. A workplace incident investigator should continue to learn and develop the skills and tools needed to undertake investigations and reflect on their own practice thoughtfully and regularly.

While much of the language in this book may reflect traditional or formal investigations, the concepts, tools, and questions are equally applicable in more collaborative approaches, such as learning teams or "new view" discussions. These approaches may avoid the word "investigation" altogether, yet they still seek to make sense of what happened, why, and how to improve.

---

[1]OHS Body of Knowledge Models of Causation: Safety 2012

Regardless of the method, the rigour of critical thinking, sense-checking, and examining credibility remains vital in group-based processes vulnerable to untested consensus or cognitive bias.

Although this book can be used as a guide to conducting an effective investigation, it is better viewed as a series of extra tools that can enhance a workplace incident investigator's existing methods and skills. This book concludes with a list of essential readings and resources that I believe are fundamental for workplace incident investigators.

The intended audience for this book is internal health and safety professionals who undertake investigations for their organisation, and work health and safety professionals who undertake investigations as external, independent workplace incident investigators. I use the term 'workplace incident investigators' to refer to both. The audience for this book may have already undertaken formal workplace incident investigation training.

While some investigation tools in this book apply equally to both internal and external investigations, others may not. This is dependent on the nature of the incident being investigated, the context in which that investigation takes place, and the discretion exercised by a competent workplace incident investigator. The workplace incident investigator should scale the investigation and the tools to the severity of the incident.

Investigation methodologies can be prescriptive, by providing a set of tools used in a logical sequence to produce a consistent outcome. There is merit in organising an investigation in this way. This book does not aim to replace or detract from those outcomes. Instead, this book aims to enhance them—whether applied within a structured model, a systems-based inquiry, or a facilitated learning conversation.

Investigation models often focus on serious incidents involving regulators, media, police, or prosecutions, although most workplace incidents do not reach this level. Workplace incident investigators can be limited by a lack of power to compel witnesses to talk and limited in their ability to obtain evidence from third parties.

By using the tools and methods in this book, a workplace incident investigator can tailor an effective investigation—or learning review—to suit the circumstances of the incident and the limitations placed upon them and still achieve meaningful findings and recommendations.

This book covers a wide range of topics essential for a broad understanding of workplace incident investigations. It explores the ethics and purpose of investigations, guiding you through each step of the incident investigation process. It considers the biases that can affect the workplace incident investigator, provides techniques for effective witness interviews and discusses the role of expert witnesses and other types of evidence. Legal considerations, such as a summary of legal professional privilege, are also covered.

This book highlights the importance of creating a Timeline of Events and confining the scope of the investigation. It explains the formation and role of the Investigation Analysis Team and introduces causation analysis based on legal principles. This book discusses the role of language, critical thinking and deductive logic in ensuring effective and meaningful investigations. Where possible, I include anecdotes and examples to assist in understanding and applying these concepts.

This book recognises the biases inherent in traditional investigation methods, understands the importance of time as a contextual factor, and acknowledges that the same adaptations leading to success can also result in failure. It advocates for a shift from a blame-oriented, single root cause paradigm to one that values inquiry, collaboration, and continuous learning. It ultimately aims to understand the broader, more complex interactions that contribute to incidents.

The language used in workplace incident investigations is more than just a means of communication; it shapes the investigation's direction, impacts its outcomes, and can reveal underlying biases. Even the term "investigation" carries connotations that may influence how the process is perceived and how participants engage with it. It suggests a formal process, often evoking images of authority, legal liability, and formal interviews, where individuals are scrutinised, potentially implying legal or professional consequences. This can hinder open and honest communication, which is essential for learning and improvement. On the other hand, referring to the process as a "learning initiative" might foster a more open environment but could fall short of stakeholders' expectations for a formal, structured process that yields clear, actionable outcomes.

With this in mind, and for the sake of clarity and consistency, I will use the following terms:

'**Causation model**' is a theoretical framework that attempts to represent and explain the causal relationships between different variables within a system, allowing workplace incident investigators to identify how one variable directly influence changes in another, essentially mapping out the "cause and effect" dynamics involved.

'**Causation methodology**' refers to the specific methods and techniques used to test and establish whether a true causal relationship exists between variables within a given workplace incident investigation.

'**Expert witness**' see the chapter on Expert Witnesses.

'**Event**' refers to any occurrence, action, or set of conditions that precedes or contributes to an incident, forming part of the sequence of circumstances analysed during a workplace incident investigation.

'**Incident**' refers to the incident or accident (see 'focus event' from AS/NZS62740:2016) as defined by the organisation or organisations involved.

'**Investigation**' refers to the investigation of an incident. Being conscious of the connotations of the word 'investigation', some may choose other terms such as 'inquiry' or 'learning' which may be better suited to the circumstances. I also recognise that for some, even the term 'inquiry' or 'learning' can also bring problematic connotations or fail to meet stakeholder expectations (while this book uses the term "investigation" for clarity and consistency, many of the ideas and tools presented can be equally useful in learning teams, debriefs, or other collaborative forms of sensemaking).

'**Organisation**' refers to the company, entity, or person in control of a business or undertaking (PCBU), to which the investigation applies.

'**Workplace incident investigator**' refers to the internal or external investigator who is investigating a work incident.

Please note that the information in this book is drawn from a variety of sources but is primarily focused on Australia and New Zealand. As a result, the content is influenced by the legal frameworks and circumstances specific to these regions.

The tools, methods, and ideas presented in this book draw on the rich body of work from many authors and practitioners, spanning not only the field of workplace safety but also disciplines such as philosophy, psychology, and law. These varied perspectives have influenced how I adapt and apply the investigation techniques outlined in this book.

I would like to acknowledge the significant contributions of these authors and practitioners. Where possible, I have made direct reference to their work or included their materials in the bibliography for further reading. In some cases, I am unable to provide a reference or source material due to the nature of the source. For this reason, I do not claim all the tools and ideas in this book as my own.

This book is not an original creation in isolation but rather a synthesis of ideas and approaches that have been tested, refined, and adapted to suit the unique challenges faced by workplace incident investigators. I hope that by incorporating these cross-disciplinary perspectives, this book offers a unique and practical guide to those tasked with the critical responsibility of conducting workplace incident investigations.

Lastly, my gratitude extends to all those whose ideas have influenced this work, knowingly or unknowingly. It is through the shared knowledge of so many that we continue to improve workplace incident investigations and create safer workplaces. Any mistakes or misinterpretations of these ideas, however, are entirely my own.

1 | Introduction

'There is no doubt that incident investigations, properly done, are one of the best avenues organisations have to understand the true state of their safety management systems.'[2]

This book covers the investigation process from incident occurrence to final recommendations. It also covers various topics related to this process, including the purpose of investigations and legal professional privilege. It also addresses the importance of acknowledging and managing bias in investigations to ensure objectivity and fairness.

Although this book outlines a structured investigation process, the tools and thinking strategies it contains can be applied just as effectively in alternative approaches to learning from work. Whether you are using a traditional formal investigation method, or a facilitated process such as a learning or safety conversation, the same foundational principles—understanding what happened, testing assumptions, exploring context, and seeking meaningful improvement—remain essential. The purpose is not to prescribe one methodology over another, but to support deeper, more reliable sensemaking regardless of the approach taken.

Investigations should be scaled to be commensurate with the severity of the incident. Specific investigation tools should be tailored to the circumstances.

Generally, the workplace incident investigation process can be divided into five phases. These phases offer a helpful structure, but the concepts within them can be scaled and adapted to suit a variety of review or inquiry formats—not all of which may be labelled an "investigation."

---

[2]Greg Smith, *Papersafe*, 2018

The first phase, **Response and Notifications**, is in Part 1 of this book. When an incident occurs, knowing what actions to take immediately, and in what order, is crucial. The workplace incident investigator must be equipped for the first incident scene visit. During this initial visit, the workplace incident investigator needs to perform specific actions to secure the scene and gather preliminary information. At this stage, the workplace incident investigator should note initial thoughts to help identify potential biases.

Moving into the second phase, **Information Gathering**, in Part 2 of this book, the focus shifts to collecting detailed evidence. This includes how to assess the competence, reliability, and credibility of witnesses, and how to interview witnesses using a variety of questioning techniques. The use of expert witnesses and specialists is also covered. Additionally, detailed information about the types of photographs needed, and consideration of the operator's manuals, guides, and other publications is discussed.

The third phase, **Data Consolidation**, is explained in Part 3 of this book. This section explains how to develop a comprehensive and reliable Timeline of Events using evidence from witness statements and authoritative sources. This phase also involves distinguishing events from the incident, identifying if there are more than one incident, focusing on the incident, and obtaining further evidence where needed.

The fourth phase, **Investigation Analysis**, covered in Part 4 of this book, is where the gathered evidence is analysed. This part includes guidance on weighting authoritative or expert opinion, applying deductive logic to the Timeline of Events, and using causation analysis to understand an incident.

Finally, the fifth phase, **Findings, Recommendations, and Reporting**, detailed in Part 5 of this book, focuses on findings and recommendations. This section explores where and why causation ends. It outlines who should be involved in a thorough analysis and how to determine effective recommendations. Additionally, it provides guidance on compiling a comprehensive investigation report.

Valuable findings that require prompt action may arise at any stage of the investigation and should be communicated immediately, without waiting for the final report. These should be promptly communicated to the organisation.

By the end of this book, you will be equipped with the knowledge and tools needed to scale and integrate effective, efficient, and ethical practices into workplace incident investigations—or any other process of organisational learning following unexpected events.

2 | Investigation Ethics

Applied professional ethics is often misunderstood in work health and safety practice, including in workplace investigations. Summarising applied professional ethics for work health and safety professionals requires a deep understanding of both normative and applied ethics.

This chapter does not seek to provide a broad overview of normative or applied professional ethics in work health and safety. It aims to provide some guidance on ethics as it may apply to work health and safety investigations. This is framed around the idea that professionals aim to do the 'right' thing, though determining what is 'right' can be unclear or difficult in specific situations. It is also important to consider what duty the profession owes to society which is different to ethical or moral duties that an individual might owe.

An example is that of a lawyer representing a client who has disclosed information about other crimes they have committed, for which there are still open investigations. Lawyers, as a profession, owe a duty to society to uphold the rule of law and justice, and they owe a duty to their client. What is the right course of action for the lawyer? Should the lawyer breach the lawyer-client privilege and inform the authorities about the confessed crimes? There are two duties in conflict here: the lawyer's duty to their client, and the lawyer's duty to society and to uphold the rule of law and justice. Ethical guidance available to lawyers makes the lawyer's professional actions clear. The legal profession's code of ethics directs lawyers to act in accordance with legal and ethical principles, even when the appropriate course of action is not immediately clear.

Unlike the legal profession, which has a well-defined hierarchy of duties—first to the administration of justice, then to the client—work health and safety professionals often operate in ethical grey areas. When investigations are conducted internally, the "client" may be the organisation itself, a particular department, or even a senior leader, making the line of accountability unclear. This lack of a defined ethical hierarchy contributes to the perception that internal investigations are vulnerable to interference or bias. Investigators must be especially deliberate in identifying who they owe duties to and in what order, particularly when those duties conflict.

While the legal profession offers clear ethical frameworks, workplace incident investigators often face similar dilemmas without the same level of structured guidance. Codes of ethics available to workplace incident investigators offer guidance such as: 'performing duties with integrity, honesty and equity' or 'be factual and accurate'. These have merit but are more accurately described as elements of a code of conduct.

Workplace incident investigators have professional duties that can conflict. Professional codes of conduct often do not address these conflicts. For instance, you cannot determine the 'right' course of action by 'being professional' or 'acting with integrity', as some codes of conduct state. The duties of workplace incident investigators could include:

- A duty to achieve the investigation's purpose and logical, meaningful findings.

- A duty to the client, their contractual obligations, and policies.

- A duty to faithfully represent witness accounts.

- A duty to ensure procedural fairness and natural justice.

- A duty to others affected by the incident (this might extend to the family of the involved person/s).

- A duty to other PCBUs and other stakeholders.

Contractual and legal limits to investigations are often overlooked or misunderstood in workplace safety contexts. Investigators may assume that their obligation to conduct a thorough investigation overrides all other considerations. However, this assumption can place them in breach of contractual agreements or legal rights. For example, the scope of an external investigator's role may be tightly defined in their contract, restricting the types of findings they can report or the parties they can engage. In labour hire or subcontractor arrangements, access to personnel and information may be limited by the commercial terms of engagement or privacy clauses. Investigators may also encounter resistance when trying to collect information held by other PCBUs who are not legally obliged to share it. In these situations, pushing forward without regard to those constraints may expose the investigator or the organisation to claims of breach of contract, privacy violations, or other legal consequences. Recognising these limits—and documenting when they impact the investigation—is not a sign of weakness or bias. It is part of acting ethically, transparently, and within one's authority.

In internal investigations, these duties can be particularly difficult to navigate because the investigator may be employed by the same organisation they are investigating. Without a clear separation between the investigative function and organisational leadership, there is a risk that the investigator's loyalty to their employer—or pressure from senior figures—may unintentionally override their ethical duty to uncover the truth, represent witness accounts accurately, or ensure procedural fairness. Unlike external investigators or professionals with clearer client relationships, internal investigators must work within this tension.

In the legal profession, duties are structured: first to the administration of justice, then to the client. This clarity supports ethical decision-making even in contentious situations. In workplace health and safety, and particularly in internal investigations, there is no comparable hierarchy. The concept of the "client" is often ill-defined—an investigator may be employed by the organisation but tasked with investigating a manager, department, or policy set by senior leadership. Without a codified professional ethic or a recognised duty of independence, investigators are left exposed to pressure and influence.

This ambiguity contributes to the frequent criticism that investigations are undermined by management interference. While external investigators can lean on contractual scope and third-party independence, internal investigators must actively define their ethical boundaries. Until the safety profession establishes a shared hierarchy of duties—such as prioritising the integrity of findings and procedural fairness above internal loyalty—investigations will remain vulnerable to these structural ethical tensions.

Some duties should be built into the methodology or process of the investigation. For example, the way witnesses are selected and managed should adhere to standards of procedural fairness and natural justice.

To navigate ethical conflicts in workplace investigations, consider the following examples of conflicting duties. It is common practice to impose an arbitrary duration on a workplace incident investigation. Sometimes, this is done contractually and in advance of any incident having occurred. The stated purpose of an imposed, arbitrary duration is that a conclusion must be reached within a pre-determined time, and the investigation must be undertaken expeditiously. While this may seem reasonable, strict adherence to arbitrary timelines can compromise the investigator's ability to fulfil the investigation's purpose and achieve meaningful findings. The arbitrary duration can produce an undesirable outcome.

If the workplace incident investigator believes the investigation's purpose and meaningful findings should prevail over an imposed duration, a conflict of duties arises that must be resolved. To systematically approach such conflicts, the following Ethical Decision-Making Model can guide investigators through complex ethical dilemmas. An example Ethical Decision-Making Model, adapted from WD Ross in *The Right and the Good*,[3] is set out below.

1. Identify the Ethical Dilemma: Clearly define the conflict between duties.

- Example: Conflict between duty to client's timeline and duty to thorough investigation.

---

[3] Ross, W.D. (1930) *The Right and the Good*. Oxford University Press.

2. Gather Information: Collect all relevant facts.

- Example: Assess the impact of an arbitrary deadline on the quality of investigation findings. Consider the time involved in obtaining evidence from third parties, such as expert witnesses and specialists.

3. Consider Ethical Principles: Apply ethical principles such as:

- Utilitarian/Consequentialist: What are the consequences of each course of action?

- Kantian: Which course of action is the 'right' course of action in its own right (without reference to the consequences).

- Intuitionist: What does the workplace incident investigator's own intuition tell them is the 'right' thing to do?

- Virtue ethics: What 'right' action does the situation call for?

4. Evaluate Alternatives: Consider how alternate courses of action affect your consideration of the ethical principles above.

- Example: Extending the timeline versus rushing the investigation.

5. Decide: Choose the option that aligns best with ethical principles and professional duties.

- Example: Decide to extend the investigation timeline to ensure meaningful findings.

6. Implement the Decision: Act on the chosen option and communicate the decision to relevant stakeholders.

- Example: Inform the client about the need for an extended timeline and its importance.

7. Review and Reflect: After implementing the decision, review the outcomes and reflect on the process.

- Example: Assess whether the extended timeline led to more meaningful findings and prevented future incidents.

Other situations where conflicting ethical duties could arise:

- Being asked to include, or pressured into including/excluding, findings or recommendations.
- Where there is only one organisation investigating, despite the obligation (legal or otherwise) being shared by all organisations connected with the incident. This can limit the workplace incident investigator's access to evidence and findings.
- Interviewing people still in shock from an incident (this could be captured indirectly by some existing codes of conduct and codes of ethics.
- Being asked, or pressured to, intrude on another's privacy without their prior consent.
- Where the organisation's policies and procedures conflict with the ethical conduct of a workplace incident investigator.
- A lack of clarity of the investigation purpose.
- A lack of transparency and awareness of (in so far as possible) biases.
- Where the investigation reveals findings not linked to the scope of the investigation but could lead to the next incident.

Workplace incident investigations are inherently complex, often involving conflicting duties to clients, affected individuals, and broader societal interests. Understanding and applying professional ethics is essential to navigate these challenges effectively. While codes of conduct provide a foundational framework, they frequently fall short in addressing the nuanced ethical dilemmas that arise during investigations. The application of structured models, such as the Ethical Decision-Making Model outlined in this chapter, equips investigators with the tools to make ethically sound decisions, fostering integrity and accountability in their investigative practices. Establishing and following a hierarchy of professional duties—like those recognised in law and medicine—may help safety professionals strengthen the ethical legitimacy and trustworthiness of their investigative work, particularly in internal contexts.

3 | Biases

Bias is a natural trait that influences decision-making, including workplace investigations. There are hundreds of recognised biases, many of which play useful roles in helping us sift through vast amounts of information to find what is relevant. Biases are present in investigations, whether the workplace incident investigator is aware of them or not. Biases can be either conscious or unconscious. They will inevitably influence an investigation and potentially make findings less effective. Consider the impact of bias in the following example.

Bias affects all investigative approaches—whether formal, regulatory, or collaborative. In fact, less structured formats like facilitated learning may be particularly vulnerable to group reinforcement, where untested assumptions or consensus can distort shared understanding. Recognising and actively challenging bias in these settings is just as important as in formal investigations.

The context for the example below comes from Anthropology. Anthropologists often study societies and cultures from both insider (emic) and outsider (etic) perspectives. Anthropologists recognise that the outsider perspective brings with it the cultural norms and biases of the outsider. Refer to this passage by anthropologist Horace Miner:[4]

> "...the culture of this people [the Nacirema] is still very poorly understood.
> They are a North American group living in the territory between the Canadian
> Cree, the Yaqui and Tarahumare of Mexico, and the Carid and Arawak of the

---

[4]Miner, H. (1956). Body Ritual Among the Nacirema. *American Anthropologist*, 58(3), 503–507

Antilles. Little is known of their origin, although traditions states that they came from the East. According to Nacirema mythology, their nation was originated by a culture hero, Notgnihsaw, who is otherwise known for two great feats of strength – the throwing of a piece of wampum across the river Pa-To-Mac and the chopping down of a cherry tree in which the Spirit of Truth resided... While much of the people's time is devoted to economic pursuits, a large part of the fruits of these labors and a considerable portion of the day are spent in ritual activity. The focus of this activity is the human body, the appearance and health of which loom as a dominant concern in the ethos of the people... The fundamental belief underlying the whole system appears to be that the human body is ugly and that its natural tendency is to debility and disease...'

What picture does this text paint in your mind? Are you imagining a pre-industrial or perhaps even a pre-agricultural tribal society? In fact, this passage is describing modern Americans—Nacirema is "American" spelled backward, and their founding hero, Notgnihsaw, is Washington reversed. The choice of words in this description reveals a deliberate bias, highlighting how language can shape perceptions.

This anthropological example illustrates how easily bias can distort perceptions.

The Pervasiveness of Bias

To help identify biases on your investigation, it is essential to:

- Be aware of the existence of biases.

- Understand the types of biases that are likely to influence investigations.

- Recognise the biases that are likely to influence you personally and your own investigations.

Everyone has biases, even those who strive to be open-minded and impartial. The notion of beginning an investigation with complete objectivity is unrealistic. No one is completely objective; we all bring our subjectivity to the table in some way.[5]

Bias affects individuals across all levels of experience and training, permeating various fields. For instance, studies of professional decision-making have shown that "criminal investigators rate witnesses as more reliable and credible when their testimony aligns with the investigator's preexisting beliefs about the case."[6]

How can you acknowledge bias as a workplace incident investigator? The key is to be considered and transparent; be familiar with the common biases that may apply to an investigation; record your thoughts at different stages of the investigation, highlighting things that may have influenced your thinking. To assist with this, a workplace incident investigator should complete an Initial Statement.

The Initial Statement

An Initial Statement should be completed as soon as possible after the incident but before beginning the investigation analysis and, ideally, before interviewing witnesses. For an in-house or internal workplace incident investigator, this means immediately after the incident is reported and the initial response is completed. For an external workplace incident investigator, it should be done right after receiving the initial brief/instructions.

The Initial Statement should include:

- The workplace incident investigator's initial assumptions about the incident and those involved in the incident.

- The workplace incident investigator's initial ideas about the causes and contributors to the incident.

---

[5]MacLean, C. L., & Dror, I. E. (2023). Measuring base-rate bias error in workplace safety investigators. Journal of safety research, 84, 108-116.

[6]MacLean, C. L., & Miller, G. S. (2024). Trust but verify: The biasing effects of witness opinions and background knowledge in workplace investigations. Journal of Safety Research, Volume 89 https://osf.io/preprints/psyarxiv/7vxu3/download

- Known and anticipated limitations, such as a limited budget, restricted access to witnesses, or delays in commencing the investigation.

- Possible conflicts of ethical duties.

Although tools like the Initial Statement are often associated with formal investigations, they can also serve a useful role in learning-based approaches by helping facilitators surface and challenge their own assumptions early in the process. This can help avoid leading the group unintentionally or overlooking alternative perspectives.

The Initial Statement can be as simple as the workplace incident investigator recording answers to the following questions:

- What do I think contributed to the incident?

- What do I think went wrong?

- Whose behaviour may have contributed to the incident?

- Why did they behave that way?

- Could the use of drugs (illicit or medical) or alcohol or both be causally relevant?

- Is the brief I received biased? Are the initial facts biased?

- How do I see this unfolding as I investigate?

- What questions should I ask the witnesses?

The Initial Statement should be revisited during the investigation, and again at the end. It may also be included in the Investigation Report.

Questions to ask towards the end of the investigation:

- What did you learn that you did not know before the investigation? Did you confirm everything you already knew, or did you learn something new?

- Why did it make sense for the person or persons to do what they did? Could you, as a workplace incident investigator, advocate for the decisions and actions of those involved?[7]

- What surprised you during the investigation?

- What would make avoiding this incident in the future extremely difficult?

- How did you make sense of conflicting information? Particularly conflicting information in witness statements?

Bias is an inherent part of human cognition that inevitably influences workplace incident investigations. By recognising its presence and understanding its diverse forms, investigators can take proactive steps to minimise its impact. Tools like the Initial Statement offer a structured method for identifying and reflecting on personal biases throughout the investigative process. This transparency strengthens the credibility of findings and ensures that investigations focus on understanding decisions within their broader context. Acknowledging that complete objectivity is unattainable encourages investigators to approach their work with humility and critical self-awareness, leading to more robust and meaningful safety outcomes. This is equally true in collaborative reviews, where the desire to reach shared understanding can obscure minority views or oversimplify complexity. Bias mitigation strategies are essential, not only to ensure fairness but to deepen the learning process itself.

---

[7] It is rare for people to act maliciously. See Thallapureddy, S et al (2023) Exploring bias in incident investigations: An empirical examination using construction case studies in *Journal of Safety Research* Vol 86

4 | Causation Modelling

'When the mental model that practitioners hold of such systems is inaccurate or incomplete, their actions may well be inappropriate. These mental models are sometimes described as "buggy".'[8]

The AS/NZS IEC 62740:2016 Root cause analysis (RCA) standard outlines a number of causation models. A causation model is a way of understanding how things happen. Causation models in workplace incident investigations can be both helpful and limiting. They guide investigators in considering aspects of an incident they might otherwise overlook but can also narrow focus too much, potentially leading to missed findings.

This book maintains the distinction between models that aid in understanding incident causation and methods used to analyse incidents as part of investigations.[9] This distinction is important. A workplace incident investigator must use their judgement in making this distinction. Depending on their knowledge of the circumstances and familiarity with various causation models, a workplace incident investigator might choose to apply one model of causation or apply multiple models of causation.

This book provides tools for causation analysis, which can also be used selectively to complement other causation analysis methods. The causation model for this causation analysis method and tools is rooted in the concept of imagining system failures as defendants in a legal case and then using legal

---

[8]Woods, D and Cook, R (1999) *Perspectives on Human Error: Hindsight Bias and Local Rationality* https://www.researchgate.net/publication/251196331_Perspectives_on _Human_Error_Hindsight_Biases_and_Local_Rationality

[9]Hollnagel, E. (2010). *FRAM Background*. Retrieved from http://sites.google.com/site/erikhollnagel2/coursematerials/FRAM_background.pdf

causation principles to perform an effective causation analysis. This method of establishing causation draws upon legal principles that have been tested and refined for hundreds of years in common law courts. System failures (as defendants) are imagined as having varying levels of culpability. Failed controls are reimagined as negligent contributors. Presumptive and proximity tests are viewed as contributory factors, and the end of the chain of causation is marked by the limits of 'reasonable foreseeability' drawn from torts law. A key advantage of legal causation is its effectiveness in handling novel circumstances. This is useful to workplace incident investigators for whom each incident presents a novel circumstance and the potential for unique findings. While this legal framework offers a powerful lens, it can also complement other approaches—such as systems thinking or narrative-based inquiry—used in learning or resilience-focused investigations.

While framing causation in this legalistic manner can be insightful, it may not always be practical or valuable for every workplace incident investigator. For this reason, workplace incident investigators should at least be familiar with several causation models. These models can be revisited throughout an investigation to support inquiry and critical thinking, but they should not be relied upon exclusively.

Hovden et al., and Dekker,[10] argue that the complexity of reality extends far beyond what any single causation model can offer. Given this complexity, it is not recommended that the workplace investigator place undue emphasis on any one causation model as the foundation for causation analysis. Many newer approaches to safety, including those informed by resilience engineering or "Safety Differently," reject linear cause-effect models altogether. These perspectives emphasise that causation is often complex, recursive, and deeply contextual. It is certainly beneficial for a workplace incident investigator to be knowledgeable about different causation models and theories. However, the workplace incident investigator should not allow these models to constrain their thinking or limit the scope of their investigation.

---

[10] Dekker, S. (2011). *Drift into Failure: From Hunting Broken Components to Understanding Complex Systems*. Surry: Ashgate.

Causation models are useful tools in workplace incident investigations, but they should be applied with discretion. Investigators must balance their understanding of these models with the flexibility to explore findings beyond a rigid framework. By scaling and adapting investigation methodologies to suit the specific circumstances of an incident, investigators can ensure a comprehensive and meaningful analysis. The ultimate objective is to identify contributing factors and broader systemic issues without being constrained by theoretical models that may oversimplify complex realities. Whether applied in formal analysis or collaborative learning conversations, causation models should support thoughtful reflection and deeper understanding—not impose artificial limits on where that understanding can go.

5 | Investigation Purpose

"If we are using an investigation model for administrative convenience without critically analysing... the purpose of incident investigation, our incident process has become bureaucratic. It is being done to follow the process, rather than to achieve a purpose."[11]

The stated purpose of an investigation significantly influences how it is conducted, including the questions posed, facts gathered, findings drawn, recommendations made, the report's structure, and the intended audience. A clear, defined purpose ensures the investigation remains focused and comprehensive, and depending on its scale, should be revisited and reaffirmed throughout. This is equally true for less formal processes, such as learning reviews or facilitated group debriefs. Without a clearly shared purpose, even well-intentioned discussions can produce vague or unfocused outcomes.

Without a clear purpose, investigations may yield inconsistent findings and incomplete information. A stated purpose keeps the workplace incident investigator on track and ensures that the investigation is thorough and relevant. Critical analysis is essential in workplace incident investigations, with the investigation's purpose being key to achieving this. In collaborative or learning-based settings, a lack of agreed purpose can also result in premature consensus or an overemphasis on storytelling without analysis. Purpose provides both focus and ethical boundaries for the inquiry.

---

[11] Greg Smith, *Papersafe*, 2018.

Consider the following examples:

Coroner's Investigation:[12]

- Purpose: As stated in section 4(2) of the Coroners Act 2006,

  '[To] *establish, so far as possible,*

    1. *that a person has died; and*
    2. *the person's identity; and*
    3. *when and where the person died; and*
    4. *the causes of the death; and*
    5. *the circumstances of the death; and*

  to make recommendations or comments under section 57A that, in the coroner's opinion, may, if drawn to public attention, reduce the chances of the occurrence of other deaths in circumstances similar to those in which the death occurred; and to determine whether the public interest would be served by the death being investigated by other investigating authorities in the performance or exercise of their functions, powers, or duties, and to refer the death to them if satisfied that the public interest would be served by their investigating it in the performance or exercise of their functions, powers, or duties."

- Findings: The coroner found "*that* [the deceased] *died on 22 August 2016 ... from non-survivable head and chest injuries sustained in a forestry incident while undertaking a line retrieval operation.*"

  The findings were concise and aligned with the Coroners Act's stated purpose.

---

[12] Brooking-Hodgson Findings. (2021). *Inquest findings into the death of Niko O'Neill Brooking-Hodgson.* Coronial Court of Rotorua, New Zealand. December 8, 2021.

Internal Bullying Investigation:

- Purpose: To determine if bullying occurred, and if so, by whom and against whom.

- Information Gathered: Primarily oral evidence from witnesses concerning various behaviours over an extended period.

- Findings: It was found that multiple definitions of bullying were simultaneously in use, and some individuals' behaviours met certain definitions but not others.

Crane Collapse Investigation:

- Purpose: To collect evidence in order to provide an incident report to the work health and safety regulator.

- Information Gathered: Focused primarily on crane stability calculations and mechanical analysis.

- Findings: The operator failed to adhere to load stability requirements and disregarded the site supervisor's directive, conducting an unauthorised crane lift.

Other Examples of Investigation Purposes

- To determine if the incident is a one-off departure from an otherwise good system of work, or indicative of systemic failures:[13] Including whether there is any evidence to support the assertion that crucial systems relevant to the incident are being managed effectively.

- Preventing a Recurrence:[14] Ensuring that similar incidents do not happen in the future.

- To Learn and Improve: Gaining insights into the task and improving processes.

---

[13]Smith, Greg (2024) *Proving Safety*.

[14]WorkSafe BC, *Reference Guide for Employer Incident Investigations* 2016. Online.

- To Obtain Legal Advice: (See the chapter on Legal Professional Privilege).

- Understanding the Physics of Machinery or Plant Failure: Investigating the mechanical aspects to prevent future failures.

- Determining whether litigation should proceed: Evaluating evidence to inform legal actions (typically the purpose of investigations conducted by workplace safety regulators).

- Fulfilling Legal Obligations: [15] Complying with regulatory requirements mandating investigations.

- Bridging the Gap Between Expected and Actual Work Practices:[16] Identifying discrepancies between how work should be done and how it is being done.

By clearly defining the purpose of an investigation from the outset, workplace incident investigators can ensure that their approach remains focused, systematic, and aligned with the investigation's objectives. A well-articulated purpose not only guides the collection and analysis of evidence but also shapes the findings and recommendations, ensuring they are meaningful, relevant, and actionable. Whether the goal is to identify systemic issues, prevent recurrence, fulfil legal obligations, or support continuous improvement, the investigation's purpose serves as the foundation for credible and effective outcomes. Ultimately, a purpose-driven investigation fosters organisational learning, and strengthens risk management practices. Whether the investigation is formal, informal, independent, or team-based, a defined purpose remains essential. It provides the shared foundation from which credible findings and meaningful learning can emerge.

---

[15] WorkSafe BC, *Reference Guide for Employer Incident Investigations* 2016. Online.

[16] Hollnagel, E., Leonhardt, J., Shorrock. S. and Licu, T. (2013). *From Safety-I to Safety-II. A White Paper*. Brussels: EUROCONTROL Network Manager.

6 | Legal Professional Privilege

"The attorney-client privilege is the oldest of the privileges for confidential communications known to the common law... Its purpose is to encourage full and frank communication between attorneys and their clients and thereby promote broader public interests in the observance of law and administration of justice."[17]

Many safety professionals hold misconceptions about how legal privilege operates, particularly concerning workplace incidents and investigations. It is important to clarify the meaning of legal professional privilege and its application in safety investigations.

What is Legal Professional Privilege?

In most common law jurisdictions, legal professional privilege protects confidential communications made for the dominant purpose of obtaining legal advice. This privilege applies to communications between a lawyer and their client, ensuring these exchanges are not subject to disclosure in legal proceedings. This confidentiality is crucial as it enables clients to communicate openly with their legal representatives, without fear that their disclosures will be used against them in court. By safeguarding these communications, legal professional privilege ensures clients receive informed legal advice and effective representation, both essential for a fair justice process. However, it's crucial to understand that not all documents or communications are protected under this privilege.

Typically, documents such as letters, reports, safe work method statements, equipment certificates, and incident investigations are not inherently cov-

---

[17]Upjohn Co. v. United States, 449 U.S. 383 (1981)

ered by legal professional privilege. If a document is not privileged, it can be "discovered" or disclosed in legal proceedings. Only communications between a lawyer and their client that fall under the scope of legal professional privilege are exempt from disclosure.

Examples to Illustrate Legal Professional Privilege

Example 1: Crane Certification

Imagine an incident occurs involving a crane tipping over on a construction site. The contract between the client organisation and the builder requires annual crane certification. Following the incident, the client requests copies of the crane certifications, but the builder refuses, citing legal professional privilege.

In this case, are the crane certifications privileged? No, they are not, because they were not created for the purpose of obtaining legal advice. Given the contract terms, it could be argued that the client owns these documents. Since the dominant purpose of the crane certifications was not to obtain legal advice, they are not protected by legal professional privilege.

Example 2: Asbestos Exposure Incident

Consider another scenario where an asbestos exposure incident occurs, potentially leading to a costly clean-up. The construction contractor contacts their lawyers within hours of the incident and begins an investigation for the purpose of obtaining legal advice. All related emails, letters, and witness statements are clearly labelled as "for the purpose of obtaining legal advice" and are stored securely, accessible only by the internal workplace incident investigator, the CEO, and the organisation's solicitors.

When the client requests a copy of the investigation, the contractor provides documents created before the day of the incident but refuses to share the witness statements, citing legal professional privilege. Here, the "dominant purpose" of the witness statements was to obtain legal advice, so they are indeed privileged and protected from disclosure.

Key Points on Legal Professional Privilege

- **Pre-Incident Documents:** In most cases, documents created prior to an incident are not covered by legal professional privilege. These documents are usually considered discoverable in legal proceedings.

- **Waiving Privilege:** Sharing legally privileged documents broadly within the organisation or with third parties may constitute a waiver of privilege, thereby forfeiting protection.

- **Purpose of the Investigation:** A workplace incident investigator must be aware of whether the investigation is intended "for the purpose of obtaining legal advice." If so, the stated purpose of the investigation should clearly reflect this. Simply stating that obtaining legal advice is the dominant purpose is insufficient; the gathered information must be shared only with legal counsel, key organisational representatives, and the workplace incident investigator.

- **Privilege Cannot Be Retroactive:** Legal professional privilege cannot be applied retroactively. This means that lawyers must be engaged before the documents are created. A workplace incident investigator cannot unilaterally create legal professional privilege after the fact.

- **Contractual and Legal Access Rights Still Apply:** Legal professional privilege does not override contractual obligations to share certain documents with other parties. For example, if a head contractor has a contractual obligation to provide safety documentation to a client, or if a principal's contract requires access to investigation records, those obligations may still apply—even if legal counsel is involved. Claiming privilege to withhold documents that were contractually required to be created or shared (e.g. pre-incident risk assessments or certifications) may not succeed and could breach the contract. Workplace incident investigators must therefore consider not only the dominant purpose test for privilege, but also whether any contractual provisions or third-party rights limit the ability to withhold documents. Misunderstanding this can result in serious commercial and legal consequences.

Balancing Confidentiality and Safety

After an incident, tension often arises between the need to share information for effective safety practices and the obligation to maintain legal privilege over certain information. A workplace incident investigator should clearly understand the organisation's objectives—whether the investigation aims to obtain legal advice or serve another purpose—and proceed accordingly.

Understanding and correctly applying legal professional privilege is crucial for any workplace incident investigator. It ensures the investigation purpose is clear, and the gathered information is appropriately protected or shared based on the organisation's legal and safety priorities. This applies not only to formal investigations but also to informal reviews, learning reviews, or debriefs. Even when the intent is collaborative or developmental, legal constraints—such as privilege, privacy rights, or contractual obligations—still apply and must be carefully considered.

7 | One-off Occurrence or Systemic Failure?

"I think one of the most straightforward things an organisation can do to obtain a better understanding of the efficacy of their workplace health and safety management systems is to include questions and observations about one-off departures v systemic failures in incident investigations".[18]

Organisations typically manage health and safety risks through a formal management system. Investigations are effective tools for testing the effectiveness of these management systems. Depending on its purpose, an investigation should aim to answer a key question: Do incidents represent isolated departures from an effective system of work, or do they indicate systemic failures within the organisation? This question may serve as the investigation's primary purpose or, at the very least, should be addressed as a key element of the investigation report. This question can serve as the primary purpose of the investigation or, at least, should be addressed as a key element within the investigation report. This key question—whether something is a one-off or symptomatic of a broader issue—sits at the heart of both formal investigations and collaborative learning methods such as learning teams. Regardless of methodology, it is a question that informs both accountability and improvement.

Gathering relevant evidence requires a structured approach, such as the PEEPO tool. Using a structured approach, the workplace incident investigator must explore several sources:

---

[18]Greg Smith (2024) *Proving Safety.*

- Expert Witnesses (as defined in the Expert Witnesses chapter): What insights can expert witnesses provide? They offer valuable perspectives on how work should be performed and what effective system adherence looks like.

- Management System: Examine the organisation's safety management system. What does it say should have happened? Is this an accurate representation of how things should happen? Was this followed in practice? This applies to both the specific incident circumstances and the overall system. For example, were weekly inspections required to be performed? What does the risk assessment say? Was this actually done?

- Witness Statements: What do the witnesses say about how the work is actually performed, the conditions they face regularly, and the specific conditions leading up to the incident? Their accounts can provide a clear picture of whether the incident was an anomaly or the result of ongoing systemic issues.

- Your Own Observations: What do your findings and direct observations suggest about the organisation's management system? Look for indicators of whether the system is functioning as intended or failing to manage risks effectively.

The key is to compare what should have happened according to the management system, what was happening from day to day under normal conditions, and what occurred at the time of the incident. Compare this information with historical incident data. This comparison also reflects principles found in learning teams and systems-based reviews, where the gap between work-as-imagined and work-as-done is explored to understand adaptations, constraints, and systemic conditions. This helps the workplace incident investigator make an informed judgement about whether the system is flawed, or the incident resulted from an unforeseeable deviation.

Causation Analysis

The causation analysis methods in this book, based on legal principles, help clarify whether the incident was an isolated occurrence or a result of systemic failure.

1. Necessary Condition: Were the events identified as necessary conditions isolated, or have similar events occurred previously? Does it occur at certain times or under certain conditions?

2. Presumptive Test: Assess whether the risk-increasing events resulted from systemic requirements, indicating a potential system failure. Were workers consistently having to use a work-around because the system was failing to address the actual work appropriately?

3. Events as Intended: Were there any events that were not as intended and were not also causally related to the incident? This is an important question to ask, as it may give a clear indication that all 'reasonably practicable steps' are not being taken and could indicate systemic issues.

Reporting Findings

When compiling the report, address whether the incident was isolated or indicative of systemic issues. The findings should directly address the question, supported by the evidence and analysis conducted during the investigation.

Recommendations should align with the investigation's findings. They must be feasible, practical, and lead to meaningful improvements in the organisation's safety practices. If systemic issues are identified, recommendations should focus on addressing them. This may involve further investigation, such as recommending an inquiry into the effectiveness of risk assessments.

- Multiple red flags missed opportunities to address known risks, or recurring safety issues may indicate systemic failures.

- Conversely, consistent compliance records and effective safety measures may indicate the incident was an isolated event.

To help answer whether the incident represents a one-off deviation or systemic failure, the investigation should rely on a thorough examination of evidence and careful causation analysis. The findings from this process will provide the necessary insight to determine whether the organisation's system of work is fundamentally sound or in need of substantial improvement. Whether these insights are surfaced through formal causation analysis or through facilitated group discussions, the goal remains the same: to understand how the system behaves under real-world pressures, and what that reveals about its resilience or fragility.

8 | The Incident Investigation Process

The incident investigation process recommended in this book consists of five main parts, aligning closely with the standards outlined in AS/NZS IEC 62740:2016. These parts are: 'Response and Notification,' 'Information Gathering,' 'Data Consolidation,' 'Analysis,' and 'Findings, Reporting, and Recommendations'. While presented as a formal structure, these phases can also be adapted and scaled to support less formal, learning-based approaches—such as learning teams or operational reviews—where the intent is to reflect, improve, and understand system behaviours without assigning blame.

The first step in the investigation process is **Response and Notification**. When an incident occurs, an immediate response may be required. The response prioritises the health and safety of both those involved and responders. The incident scene is then secured and preserved to maintain its integrity for investigation. Notifications may include reporting to authorities such as the police, the work health and safety regulator, or the environmental authority, depending on the nature of the incident. The organisation may also need to notify insurers, clients, and other stakeholders. The investigation's purpose is defined, and the workplace incident investigator completes an initial statement to address potential limitations, ethical concerns, or biases.

The second phase is **Information Gathering**, where comprehensive data collection takes place. This involves obtaining witness statements and expert witness statements, as well as the workplace incident investigator's own observations about the witnesses. Photographs of the scene, along with relevant procedures, policies, guidance documents, manuals, references, and other materials, are collected. The equipment involved in the incident is examined, and samples, such as contaminated food samples, are collected and analysed. The incident history is reviewed to identify any similar past incidents that could provide context or insights into the current investigation. External specialists may be engaged for data collection and analysis.

In the third phase, **Data Consolidation**, the investigator compiles a detailed Timeline of Events covering the period before and after the incident. This Timeline of Events establishes a chronology based on evidence to aid understanding of the circumstances of the incident. The frequency of related incidents is assessed to determine whether the incident was isolated or part of a recurring pattern.

The fourth phase, **Analysis**, involves a thorough examination of the consolidated data. The incident is confined to ensure a clear focus, and it is determined if there is more than one incident involved. An investigation team is assembled, and an analysis meeting scheduled. During this phase, causation is determined through deductive logic and consensus. The organisation's sphere of influence is assessed to determine findings and inform recommendations. Recommendations are prioritised, resourced, and articulated clearly to ensure they are actionable and effective.

The final phase, **Findings Reporting and Recommendations**, involves compiling a comprehensive report that includes the outcomes of the analysis. This report details the findings, causation, and recommendations. The investigator revisits and updates the initial statement to incorporate new insights, ethical considerations, and limitations identified during the investigation.

By following this structured incident investigation process, organisations can ensure a thorough and objective examination of incidents, leading to meaningful findings and recommendations. Even in collaborative settings, using a scaled version of this structure can bring clarity, rigour, and consistency to group-based learning or incident reflection processes.

Part 1
Response and Notification

9 | Initial Response and Notification

A safety advisor whose role involved oversight of kitchen operations, received a call from one of the kitchens. A chef reported that the kitchen was "on fire." In shock, the safety advisor repeated the question for confirmation: "The kitchen is on fire?!" The chef responded, "Yes." Instructions were given immediately: "Don't hesitate. Activate the fire alarm and evacuate the area. Consider using the fire extinguishers or fire blanket if appropriate, but only if it is safe to do so. Otherwise, evacuate. Emergency services will be contacted."

When the safety advisor arrived at the scene, there was little evidence of smoke or fire, only a group of confused chefs at the muster location. The chef who had made the call was approached and asked to describe the fire. They explained that they had observed a "fire" on the BBQ. When asked if they meant that fat from the meat had caused a momentary "flash" flame, they confirmed this was the case. It was pointed out that this was quite different from describing the situation as "the kitchen is on fire." The chef insisted that, in the moment, their description felt appropriate.

In hindsight, it was fortunate that the safety advisor had erred on the side of caution by advising the fire alarm to be activated. This situation highlighted how one person's "kitchen on fire" could just be a BBQ flare.

Accurate information is crucial during the initial response to an incident, and how facts are communicated is equally important. When describing an incident, it's essential to consider how your wording will paint a picture in the mind of the reader or listener. Avoid subjective language such as 'serious,' 'major,' or 'minor,' as these terms lack specificity. Instead, focus on describing the facts clearly and precisely. For example, rather than saying "the worker suffered a serious cut," describe the injury in detail: "The involved person (IP) received a 5cm laceration (approximately 3mm deep) to their right hand while using a skill saw that kicked back after hitting a knot in the timber. The IP was not wearing gloves and required three stitches." Similarly, use neutral language like 'contacted' instead of emotive terms such as 'smashed into' or 'crashed into'. The language used in the early stages of a response can shape perceptions and bias future analysis. Descriptive, factual communication is not only more accurate—it also supports more credible learning and investigation outcomes, regardless of methodology.

As a workplace incident investigator, you may receive phone calls reporting incidents. Your response in such situations is critical. It should be calm and measured, providing reassurance to the caller who may be experiencing fear, anxiety, panic, or stress. Avoid making or repeating assumptions about causation, blame, or intent at this early stage. Doing so can inadvertently shape the narrative, limiting the openness or objectivity of subsequent learning or analysis. Your response should prioritise the following areas (in order):

1. People:

- First, determine if anyone is hurt and whether they are receiving the right medical attention. Assess if it is safe for others to assist them. If necessary, instruct the caller to hang up and contact emergency services, (or offer to do so on their behalf) and calling them back once this is done. To do this effectively, workplace incident investigators involved in initial responses should be trained in first aid, emergency response, and mental health first aid.

- There are important first aid considerations to keep in mind. Note: This is not an exhaustive list, and first aid guidelines are regularly updated. It is essential to ensure your knowledge remains current and aligned with best practices.

○ Burns: For any incident involving a burn, the affected area should be flushed with cold running water for at least 20 minutes, then covered with clear plastic wrap if available.

○ Electric Shock: In many instances, a person who has received an electric shock is at potential high risk of a heart attack within the next 24 hours. They should seek medical attention and potentially undergo an electrocardiogram (ECG) to monitor for heart palpitations.

○ Air Embolism: Any incident involving a substance under pressure (such as using compressed air) that penetrates the skin should be treated as a medical emergency. The person should go to a hospital immediately.

2. Property:

• Assess if anything is damaged and if there is a risk of further damage (such as from a spill continuing to spread) unless immediate action is taken. Make the scene safe, provided it does not endanger additional people, property, or the environment.

3. Incident Scene Preservation:

• Once medical aid has been provided and the risk of further damage is mitigated, it is important to preserve the incident scene for investigation. The actions taken to preserve the incident scene will vary greatly from incident to incident.

• Incident scenes can vary greatly, and therefore it is very difficult to provide guidance that would apply to all. Some things to consider are:

○ Protect the scene from people: Secure the area around the incident by putting up barricade tape or other physical barriers to prevent people from walking into the area.

○ Protect the scene from weather: protective plastic covers or similar might serve this purpose.

- Protect items from oxidation (e.g., rust or discolouration) using protective wrapping or shelter. These items may need to be removed.

- Where the scene or items cannot be protected, ensure photographs of the scene or item are comprehensive. Refer to the chapter on Photographs.

4. Reporting:

- Consider who is currently aware of the incident and who else needs to be informed. Identify whether a regulator or relevant authority needs to be notified.

- When reporting, stick to the facts. If you do not have certain information, state that you do not know. Choose your words carefully to prevent misunderstandings. For instance, the term "electrocution" can mean both "electric shock" and "death by electric shock," so precise language is crucial. Providing accurate information promptly can prevent misinformation and reduce the time spent on corrections.

- Avoid terms like "minor" or "major" when describing injuries. Different people may interpret these words differently. As previously mentioned, provide a clear description, such as "The injury is a laceration approximately 5mm deep and 50mm long across the left forearm. Bleeding has stopped."

There are additional considerations to keep in mind during the initial response:

- Offering Trauma Counselling and Support: Ensure trauma counselling and support are available to those affected. Training in mental health first aid (as well as first aid) for a workplace incident investigator should be a minimum.

- Supporting Others Affected: Consider the impact on other workers, family members, and the community, and arrange support for them if possible. In some cases, financial assistance may be appropriate and should be discussed with the organisation and its professional advisers (e.g., legal counsel).

- Drug and Alcohol Testing: Determine whether drug and alcohol testing is appropriate, as it may be required by organisational policies. The workplace incident investigator should note the causal relevance of drug and alcohol testing in the Initial Statement.

Remember that a workplace incident may also constitute a crime or offence, requiring notification to relevant government agencies. Consider whether the incident needs to be reported to:

- The Police (e.g., road traffic incidents, assault, drugs).

- The work health and safety regulator (if it is a notifiable incident).

- An environmental protection authority (e.g., in the case of environmental spills or releases).

- A marine authority (if relevant).

- Other government agencies (e.g., Privacy Commissioner).

- Other clients or private bodies under statutory obligation.

- Your insurer or your organisation's insurers.

An organisation should have a clear and effective reporting process in place. As an internal workplace incident investigator, you should be notified as soon as possible after an incident, ideally after first aid and scene securing have been addressed. The incident notification and reporting process should facilitate early intervention. Active participation in the reporting process and subsequent investigation should be an employment requirement of workers and a contractual requirement of contractors.

By following these guidelines, an organisation and workplace incident investigator can lay the groundwork for a thorough and successful investigation.

Part 2
Information Gathering

10 | Initial Evidence

Collecting evidence during an incident investigation can present several challenges. Firstly, the relevance of evidence is not always immediately apparent. What may seem initially insignificant or irrelevant could later prove to be very important. Furthermore, the incident scene may have been disturbed before the workplace incident investigator arrives, potentially resulting in the loss of critical evidence. For example, individuals involved in the incident may have left the scene, either because they were taken to hospital or departed voluntarily.

Balancing the Scope and Severity of the Investigation

The scale and seriousness of the investigation will often influence the level of investment in the resources used to gather evidence. Workplace incident investigators must strike a balance between their duty to achieve the investigation's purpose and meaningful findings, and the constraints posed by contractual obligations and organisational policies and resources. This balance is just as relevant in reflective or learning-based reviews, where gathering a proportionate amount of evidence still supports meaningful insights without overwhelming participants or losing focus.

Workplace incident investigators must also be mindful of contractual limitations when collecting evidence, particularly in multi-party worksites involving contractors, subcontractors, or third parties. Some documentation, tools, or materials at the scene may be governed by commercial agreements that restrict access or sharing. For example, an investigator may wish to inspect a subcontractor's proprietary method statements, photographs, or data logs. However, the subcontractor may be contractually entitled to withhold this information from the principal contractor or external parties unless explicitly permitted in the contract. Similarly, accessing shared client-contractor documents—like system logs or crane certifications—may require prior consent. Investigators must not assume a safety investigation automatically overrides these legal or contractual boundaries. The goal is to gather as much relevant evidence as possible while adhering to practical, ethical, and contractual constraints.

The collection of evidence might also need to be scaled to the severity of the incident. An incident involving one or more serious injuries, multiple persons, and/or a high remedial cost would require a comprehensive evidence search. In contrast, an incident with minor consequences and straightforward circumstances may require only basic evidence collection. The scaling of evidence collection, and the use of the tools to collect that evidence, will depend on the requirements of the organisation and the expectations of stakeholders.

Despite these challenges and expectations, there are several key types of evidence that a workplace incident investigator should prioritise:

1. Contemporaneous Notes: Notes made by the workplace incident investigator while observing the incident scene are invaluable (see the chapter on photographs and the use of action video cameras). These notes capture the initial impressions and details that may not be apparent later.

2. Weather Reports: If weather conditions are relevant to the incident, it is important to obtain a weather report as soon as possible. Refer to the official meteorological bureau's website to obtain weather data for the relevant day, week, or longer period.

3. Samples and Specimens: Depending on the nature of the incident, collecting physical evidence such as dust swab samples, food samples, product or waste samples, and water or air samples can provide critical insights during the investigation. These samples should be correctly

labelled and securely stored to preserve their integrity. This may require specialist assistance.

4. Load Restraint or Dropped Object Incidents: For incidents involving load restraint or dropped objects, it's essential to gather information on the size, weight, and dimensions of the object, its centre of gravity, the distance it fell, and details of any restraints used. Tools such as a 'dropped objects calculator' can help determine the forces involved in the incident.

5. Photographs: Photographs are a vital component of evidence collection, though it can be challenging to anticipate which images will be needed later. In addition to obvious photographs of the tools, materials, and location involved, it's important to take photographs that provide context. Refer to the chapter on photographs for more information.

6. Topographical Maps and Street Views: If relevant, it's useful to obtain topographical screenshots and views of the street from online photographic maps. This can provide additional context to the incident. If available, a drone can be used to capture topographical photographs of the incident scene.

Essential Tools for Initial Incident Response

While an online search can provide a comprehensive list of items for workplace incident investigators, the following essentials are particularly useful during initial incident responses:

- Notepad and Pen: For making contemporaneous notes by the workplace incident investigator.

- Plastic Zip Lock/Sealable Bags: For collecting samples.

- Water Wipes: Useful for collecting some types of swab samples.

- Camera with Spare Batteries and Memory Cards: Depending on the incident, the camera may need to be intrinsically safe.

- Photo Scale Reference: A ruler or coin can serve as a scale reference in photographs.

- Recording Device with Spare Batteries and Memory Cards: Excellent for capturing witness interviews and recordings of oral contemporaneous notes.

- Tape Measure (up to 50 meters): Useful for measuring distances relevant to the incident.

- Copies of Useful Forms: Including statement forms and reporting forms. A checklist of evidence types can serve as a useful aide-mémoire.

- Disposable Gloves: For handling evidence safely.

- High Visibility Barrier Tape: To demarcate the incident scene.

- Action Camera: This can be worn by the investigator to record footage while inspecting the site.

- Apps for Measuring Light and Noise: While not comprehensive or certified, smartphone apps can provide initial indicators of light and noise levels. If these factors are likely to be causative, a certified operator should be called to take formal measurements. App-derived measurements should not replace formal measurements conducted by certified professionals when regulatory compliance is required.

- Scales: Portable scales are particularly useful for incidents involving small, dropped objects or load restraint failures.

Organising evidence effectively is crucial for guiding the investigator through analysis, ensuring no critical information is overlooked. One widely recognised method for structuring evidence is the PEEPO tool, used in popular investigation methods. PEEPO stands for People, Environment, Equipment, Procedures, and Organisation, providing a systematic approach to obtaining, categorising, and analysing evidence. Regardless of the method used, methodical evidence organisation enables investigators to maintain a comprehensive search for evidence. Frameworks like PEEPO can also be used to guide discussions in group-based or learning team settings, helping ensure a shared, structured exploration of contributing factors—even in less formal or non-blame approaches.

The collection and organisation of evidence are fundamental to conducting a thorough and effective incident investigation. The scale of evidence collection should align with the severity of the incident, with higher-risk cases necessitating more extensive documentation and analysis. Given the complexities of workplace incidents, investigators should adopt a structured approach, not only in gathering relevant evidence but also in organising it systematically. Tools like the PEEPO framework help categorise evidence in a way that supports logical analysis, enabling investigators to identify causal relationships and systemic issues efficiently. By prioritising key evidence types—such as contemporaneous notes, environmental conditions, physical samples, and photographic records—investigators can construct a robust and well-supported account of the incident.

11 | Witness Interviews — Oral Evidence

"Doveryai, no proveryai"

– Russian proverb that translates as "trust but verify"[19]

Oral evidence holds a unique and vital position in workplace incident investigations, offering insights that no other form of evidence can provide. Unlike documents or physical artifacts, oral evidence provides a dynamic narrative that reflects not just the events but the motivations, perceptions, and biases of those involved. This form of evidence is deeply rooted in legal traditions across common law jurisdictions. It is invaluable for its ability to reveal information through direct interaction. Observing a witness's demeanour, tone, and choice of words allows investigators to assess credibility and reliability in ways that static, documented evidence cannot. Oral evidence forms a critical link between written records and human experience, ensuring that it does not exist in isolation but contributes to a cohesive understanding of an incident. When treated with the attention it deserves, oral evidence can uncover systemic issues, guide meaningful lessons, and foster a culture of trust and accountability—essential elements for preventing future incidents. Therefore, taking effective witness statements is a key skill for any workplace incident investigator. This applies equally in learning-focused investigations where multiple participants contribute to a shared understanding. In these contexts, unverified assumptions and groupthink can obscure the facts unless partic-

---

[19]MacLean, C. L., & Miller, G. S. (2024). Trust but verify: The biasing effects of witness opinions and background knowledge in workplace investigations. Journal of Safety Research, Volume 89 https://osf.io/preprints/psyarxiv/7vxu3/download

ipants' accounts are approached with curiosity, respectful challenge, and critical reflection.

A witness statement is essentially recorded oral evidence. Oral evidence has been highly valued for centuries. The importance of oral evidence is reflected in the ancient commandment, 'Thou shalt not bear false witness'. Even today, oral evidence remains central to most legal systems around the world.

In the English common law tradition, all evidence must be introduced through a witness who has sworn or affirmed to tell the truth. Written evidence must, therefore, be supported by oral testimony. For example, a completed pre-start inspection checklist for a vehicle is evidence, but evidence of what? Can we say, based on the document alone, that each item on that checklist was *actually* checked? Only a witness can verify this. This is often done through an affidavit or by the witness attending court and undergoing examination in chief and cross-examination. If a document is not introduced through oral testimony, or if the testimony is undisputed, the document may not be admitted as evidence.

A notable example of this is the case of *Moore v SD Tillett Memorials Pty Ltd [2002] SAIRC 47*, where a prosecution was successfully defended without any written evidence being considered; the defence was successful due to oral evidence. Where documents are required as evidence, they are tendered through a witness's affidavit. This establishes a crucial link between the document and the oral evidence.

Despite its importance, workplace incident investigators often overemphasise documentary evidence, which can undermine the investigation. Oral statements provide rich insights into a witness's state of mind, reliability, engagement, memory, and biases. They also provide a broader narrative from which an organisation can learn valuable lessons. This is true not only in formal investigations but also in collaborative learning settings. Even where the goal is not to assign blame, assessing the plausibility, internal consistency, and limitations of witness accounts remains a vital part of understanding what happened and why.

The Value of Oral Evidence

Oral evidence is highly regarded in common law jurisdictions. This is because:

- A person is more likely to tell the truth if they testify under oath and face the possibility of perjury if they lie.

- Falsehoods in a witness's account are more likely to be exposed during cross-examination.

- Judges and juries are better equipped to assess a person's credibility when they can observe the witness's demeanour in court.

While witnesses in a safety investigation are not subject to oaths or perjury, a workplace incident investigator can still glean a great deal from a witness's demeanour. Cross-examination questioning techniques can be particularly useful in discerning the reliability of a witness.

The process of interviewing witnesses should involve qualifying witnesses, recording their statements, managing interviews effectively, and applying appropriate questioning techniques. The scale of the investigation and the severity of the incident will determine the depth and detail of the witness statements collected.

12 | Witness Interviews — Qualifying Witnesses

Qualifying witnesses is a critical step in ensuring the reliability of evidence in workplace incident investigations. Witnesses provide valuable insights into the events and context of an incident; however, their accounts must be evaluated for competence, relevance, and credibility. Not all oral evidence from witnesses carries equal weight and understanding how to assess and manage these weightings is key to building a sound investigation. This chapter explores practical approaches to qualifying witnesses, addressing challenges such as bias, trauma, and conflicting accounts to help investigators gather evidence that is both useful and trustworthy. This process is just as important in learning-oriented or collaborative investigations. In these contexts, where group narratives can emerge, evaluating whether participants are providing direct, reliable insights—or are repeating second-hand or assumed information—is essential to avoid bias and groupthink.

In common law jurisdictions, witnesses must be qualified to give evidence based on several criteria:

1. Competence: A witness is considered competent when they may lawfully be called to give evidence. In most jurisdictions, everyone is deemed competent unless they are mentally disabled or impaired to the extent that they do not understand the nature of their statement, or if they are a child under 12 years of age. A witness may also be temporarily deemed incompetent if suffering from trauma or shock related to the incident.

2. Compellability: A compellable witness is one who is legally obliged to give evidence. Exceptions to this include legal privileges, such as spousal privilege. In legal proceedings, a compellable witness can be subpoenaed to testify.

3. Credibility/Reliability: A credible witness is one who is telling the truth or has a sound recollection of events and the incident. In legal proceedings, judges or juries decide whether a witness's evidence will be considered 'factual'. In a workplace incident investigation, credibility is assessed after the statement is taken, with the workplace incident investigator responsible for making this judgement.

4. Relevance: A witness must be relevant to the investigation. This means their evidence should be based on what they directly saw, heard, smelled, tasted, or touched. Expert witnesses (as defined in this book) are also considered relevant. Evidence based on hearsay or speculation—where it was not directly seen, heard, smelled, touched, or tasted—is considered weak. Hearsay, which is an out-of-court statement offered for its truth, is generally inadmissible in court unless an exception applies. Speculation occurs when a witness draws conclusions without objective facts, which is unhelpful in an investigation.

Qualifying witnesses in workplace incident investigations helps avoid taking statements from individuals who did not directly experience the incident - what might be called a 'false witness'. While hearsay may be used if the person who made the statement is unavailable, it remains weak evidence and should be avoided when possible.

Challenges in Witness Qualification

Witness qualification is rarely an issue in workplace incident investigations, though it remains an important consideration. You may encounter situations where a witness is:

- Traumatised: The witness may struggle or be unable to give a statement due to trauma or the effects of the incident.

- Protected by Privilege: The witness may be subject to or protected by legal professional privilege or other rules, rendering them unwilling or unable to participate in an interview.

- Fearful: The witness may be afraid to participate in an interview.

A workplace incident investigator lacks the legal authority to compel witnesses. If a witness is unwilling or unable to provide evidence, the workplace incident investigator must accept this, report it to the commissioning organisation, document it as part of the evidence-gathering process, and proceed with the investigation without that witness's interview evidence. This should be documented in the workplace incident investigator's own statement about that witness. Some organisations include clauses in employment agreements requiring employees to provide statements if they witness an incident. Although not enforceable in all jurisdictions, such clauses can encourage reluctant witnesses to share their accounts of the incident. While formal compellability is not a factor in learning teams or participatory investigations, the need to test whether a person's account is based on direct observation (rather than speculation or hearsay) remains essential to the credibility of the findings.

Expert Witnesses

The qualification of expert witnesses follows similar principles and will be addressed in a later chapter.

By understanding the importance and criteria for qualifying witnesses, workplace incident investigators can gather reliable, relevant evidence, leading to more accurate and effective investigations.

13 | Witness Interviews — Statements

Having discussed what a witness statement is, why it is important, and who should provide it, the next steps involve understanding when, where, and how to take these statements effectively.

When to Take a Witness Statement

Witness statements should be taken as soon as possible after the incident. Human memory is inherently fallible and deteriorates quickly. As one study notes:

> *"Because the contents of our memories for experiences involve the active manipulation (during encoding), integration with pre-existing information (during consolidation), and reconstruction (during retrieval) of that information, memory is, by definition, fallible at best and unreliable at worst."*[20]

Although a workplace incident investigator may require time to prepare before taking a statement, they should avoid excessive delays in the process. Workplace incident investigators can often return to obtain follow-up statements if required. However, it is important to be mindful that delay can affect a witness's recollection and the overall duration of the investigation.

---

[20] Howe ML, Knott LM. The fallibility of memory in judicial processes: lessons from the past and their modern consequences. *Memory*. 2015;23(5):633-656. doi:10.1080/09658211.2015.1010709

Where to Take a Witness Statement

The location for taking a witness statement can vary, but there are key considerations to ensure the environment is conducive to open and honest recollections:

- Noise: Ensure that the location is quiet and free from interruptions. The setting should allow the witness to speak comfortably without distractions.

- One Witness at a Time: To avoid any potential collusion or contamination (intentional or unintentional) of the witness's recollection of events, it is important to interview witnesses individually. This may influence the choice of location.

- Privacy: Consider the witness's need for privacy, especially if they are sharing sensitive or personal information. They should feel secure that their conversation will not be overheard by others.

Witnesses may also wish to have a support person present (some jurisdictions require an organisation to allow a support person to attend, if it is requested by the witness), and the workplace incident investigator may want someone to assist by taking notes. These factors will influence the selection of the interview location and scheduling. The support person or advocate should not be another witness.

How to Take Witness Statements - Before the Interview

Before conducting the witness statement interview, it is important to prepare adequately:

- Use a Standard Template: Have a template ready that can prompt the capture of essential information. The essential information may include:
  - An account of events in chronological order.
  - A diagram to indicate the location of any injury on a human figure.

- A set of standard questions to collect basic information such as the witness's name and the date of the interview.

- A blank area for the witness to draw, or for the workplace incident investigator to draw under their direction, a diagram or other relevant image of the incident.

- A space for the witness's signature or initials on each page.

- Arrange a time and place: As stated above, organise a time and place to speak to the witness. The workplace incident investigator should allow for a support person or advocate and determine whether an audio recording of the interview is required.

- Allow ample time: Allocate sufficient time for the interview, as it may exceed two hours. While this may seem lengthy, a thorough witness statement is essential for reliable evidence.

- Avoid Pre-Written Questions: Pre-writing questions can restrict the workplace incident investigator's flexibility. Situations are often too diverse for pre-prepared questions to remain effective. Instead of thinking about specific questions, think about the key outcomes being sought from the interview: these can change as the interview progresses, which in turn means the questions will change.

- Familiarise Yourself with Witness Management Techniques: Review the techniques outlined in the chapter on Witness Management to prepare for managing the interview effectively.

During the Interview

While conducting the witness statement interview, keep the following principles in mind:

- Explain: Explain the purpose of both the interview and the investigation to the witness. Explain that the information of interest is what the witness saw, what the witness heard, what the witness did. In other words, they are only being asked to recall things they directly observed.

Early candour and openness by the workplace incident investigator about what is expected can set the witness at ease.

- Suspend Judgement: Avoid making judgements or using judgemental language during the interview.

- Maintain Humility: Maintain a humble, inquisitive, and approachable demeanour. Build rapport with the witness by making them feel comfortable and at ease. Keep the tone cooperative and friendly. Witness interviews can be intimidating, so the workplace incident investigator's demeanour should be polite, professional, and friendly. It is important to place the witness at ease throughout the process.

- Acknowledge Bias: The workplace incident investigator should consider how their questions are worded. While it's impossible to eliminate bias, the workplace incident investigator should acknowledge any potential biases before entering the room. Bias can subtly influence the framing and delivery of questions. If you find yourself leading the witness, pause, reassess, and rephrase the question.

- Offer Support: The witness may be experiencing post-incident trauma or be showing signs of unease. If this becomes apparent during the interview, pause the interview and address it. This might involve referring them to a suitable counselling service. If a potential mental health injury is identified, stop the interview to arrange professional assistance. Resume the interview only when a qualified medical practitioner deems the witness mentally fit to proceed.

- Recording: If you choose to record the interview, ask for the witness's permission first. Audio recordings are useful but not always necessary. If the witness declines to be recorded, respect their choice and take notes instead.

- Use Questioning Techniques: Employ the questioning techniques outlined in the subsequent chapters.

- Chronological Order: Ensure the statement is in chronological order, capturing all relevant events and timelines. Depending on the incident, you may need to go back further in time as the narrative unfolds, and other details become relevant. Depending on the witness's recollection, gaps in the chronology may require revisiting.

- Slow Down if Necessary: Pause the interview if needed to ensure accurate notetaking. Ensure the witness's narrative covers all relevant events. If gaps exist, guide them to revisit earlier details.

- Review the Statement: Review the statement with the witness to confirm accuracy and clarify any outstanding points. Upon completion, advise the witness if the statement requires revision. Allow them to review the final draft before finalisation.

- Finalise the Statement: Have the witness sign the completed statement at the end of the interview, including the date and time of the signature. If multiple pages are involved, ensure the witness initials each page. All amendments should be initialled by both the workplace incident investigator and the witness.

- Plan for Follow-Up: Seek permission to follow up on their statement if necessary. As you gather and collate more information, you may need additional details or clarification.

After the Interview

After the witness statement interview, it is important to take the following steps:

- Revise the Statement if Necessary: If the statement requires revision, share the final draft with the witness before finalising it.

- Document Your Observations: As soon as possible after taking the witness statement, record your observations regarding the interview. Although often overlooked, the workplace incident investigator's statement is crucial, providing insights into the witness's reliability, credibility, and evidence assessment. Your statement should address:

- Your qualifying of the witness.

- The witness's demeanour during the interview.

- Your thoughts on the witness's reliability and credibility.

- Any biases the witness may have.

- Whether you think the witness has colluded with others.

- The weight you give to their evidence (e.g., the witness may be credible, but their account may be unreliable for reasons such as physical distance from the incident).

These observations are just as important in participatory or learning team investigations, where there may be less formal documentation but just as much need to reflect on the quality and weight of what was said.

By thoughtfully determining when, where, and how to obtain witness statements, a workplace incident investigator can ensure the collection of accurate and reliable evidence, essential for a thorough and effective investigation.

14 | Witness Interviews — Witness Management

"[A] person's nonverbal behaviour has more bearing than his words on communicating feelings or attitudes to others." [21]

Creating a comfortable and trusting environment is essential for successful witness interviews in workplace incident investigations. When witnesses feel at ease and have a good rapport with the workplace incident investigator, they are more likely to be cooperative and share valuable information. Conversely, if a witness feels threatened, defensive, accused, or uncomfortable, they are much less likely to open-up and may withhold important information. Sometimes, creating an informal atmosphere during the interview can lead to a better experience for the witness and more valuable information for the investigator. Trust and openness enable deeper insights, no matter the investigative approach.

Addressing Trauma

After an incident, some witnesses may be experiencing post-incident trauma which may impact their ability to provide accurate statements. As mentioned earlier in the context of witness competence, there are additional considerations when dealing with traumatised individuals. A workplace incident investigator should ideally have training in identifying mental health issues. This training can help assess a witness's competence or, at the very least, identify potential signs of trauma and distress. If nothing else, where signs of

---

[21] Mehrabian, A (1971) *Silent Messages*. University of California

mental health issues are identified the workplace incident investigator should be competent enough to refer the person to appropriate care services.

Understanding Body Language

Body language is a powerful communication tool, often conveying much of the message beyond spoken words. Recognising body language cues can help determine whether someone is comfortable during an interview. For those proficient in observing these cues, body language may also suggest when a person is being dishonest.

Chase Hughes, in *The Ellipses Manual*, emphasises that a single body language cue is not definitive. For example, a person may cross their arms because they are becoming defensive, or they may do so simply because they feel cold. The real power of body language observation comes from noticing *clusters* of cues. For instance, if a person leans forward in their chair, points their torso toward you, and keeps their palms open, these combined cues suggest they are comfortable, truthful, and open at that moment.

Defensive cues

These non-verbal cues may suggest that a witness is experiencing psychological discomfort or hesitancy. Importantly, no single behaviour confirms dishonesty — but multiple cues at the same time may indicate the need for rapport-building or a change in interview approach:

- Protective gestures (crossing arms, shielding neck or torso, grasping personal items).

- Physical withdrawal (leaning away, shrinking posture, hiding feet).

- Facial tension (tightened jaw, pursed lips, furrowed brow).

- Repetitive or unconscious movements (tapping fingers, fiddling with objects, rubbing hands).

- Changes in voice tone or speed (elevated pitch, faster speech, long pauses before answering).

- Non-responsiveness or indirect answers (deflecting, vague phrasing, unusual formality or excessive politeness).

- Disruptive mirroring (witness begins asking you questions or shifts into a performance mode).

If you notice a witness displaying multiple cues at the same time, it may be time to adjust your interview technique to make them more comfortable. Consider pausing the interview, offering a drink, rescheduling, or taking a break to share an anecdote and build rapport. Resume the interview once you observe that the witness's body language has returned to a more relaxed state.

Verbal dishonesty cues

Certain verbal cues may suggest that a witness is being dishonest:

- Delays before answering, especially after straightforward questions.

- Unusual word choices or euphemisms that downplay events (e.g., "borrowed" instead of "took").

- Increased pitch or sudden speed in delivery, possibly to deflect or rush the exchange.

- Answers that miss the question entirely or feel rehearsed (e.g., listing qualifications instead of describing actions).

- Absence of ownership in language, such as avoiding "I" or "we" when describing what happened.

- Overly formal or oddly polite language shifts, particularly when the tone doesn't match earlier conversation.

- Minimising qualifiers like "basically," "probably," or "as far as I know," especially when added to specific questions.

- Repeated apologies or expressions of helplessness that might deflect scrutiny ("Sorry, I didn't really see much").

- Counter-questioning, where the witness starts asking the investigator questions in return.

If you notice more than one of these verbal cues occurring at the same time, take a moment to consider what was being discussed and how it might relate to potential dishonesty. Then, implement appropriate questioning techniques from the Questioning Techniques chapter to probe further.

Comfort cues

These behaviours may suggest a witness is engaged, cooperative, and comfortable sharing accurate information:

- Relaxed posture with openness (uncrossed limbs, visible palms, elbows away from body).

- Congruent gestures (hand gestures that match speech rhythm or emphasis).

- Genuine emotional displays (smiling that involves the eyes, eyebrow raises in surprise, reflective pauses).

- Recollection behaviours (looking upward or to the side when recalling details, touching chin while thinking).

- Comfort-based movements (adjusting furniture, removing shoes, playful foot gestures).

If you observe multiple cues at the same time, it suggests that the witness is relaxed and likely being truthful. Mimicking or matching their body language can further reinforce this rapport.

Your Demeanour While Conducting an Interview

As a workplace incident investigator, it is your responsibility to ensure that the witness feels comfortable and safe during the interview. Consider the interview's setting, including the room's location, furniture arrangement, and temperature. Your clothing should be appropriate and reasonably aligned with the witness's attire. For example, do not wear a formal suit and tie if the witness is in high-visibility clothing, having just come from a construction site. The atmosphere should be casual and relaxed.

Presenting an open and honest demeanour is crucial for building trust with the witness. Avoid displaying discomfort cues and instead use comfort cues while conducting the interview. Be transparent about the purpose of the interview and investigation.

Using Inquisitive Language

The language you use during the interview should be inquisitive rather than accusatory. For example:

- Accusatory: "You weren't wearing a hard hat, were you?"

- Inquisitive: "I noticed you aren't wearing a hard hat. Is everything okay?"

The first question is framed as an accusation and is likely to make the witness defensive. A better approach is to ask questions in a way that invites the witness to share their perspective without feeling attacked or accused.

Consider another example:

- Accusatory: "Why did you do that?"

- Inquisitive: "How did you come to that decision?"

Asking "why" questions can put the witness on the defensive. Instead, use less confrontational language by focusing on the process or reasoning behind their actions. This shifts the focus away from blaming the witness and towards understanding what they saw, heard, felt, and experienced.

Dealing with Hostile Witnesses

Despite your best efforts, some witnesses may be hostile: disruptive or unwilling to cooperate. Hostile witnesses often display strong body language cues indicating discomfort, deception, or contempt towards the workplace incident investigator. The techniques outlined in this chapter can help prevent such situations. If these fail, it may be best to terminate the interview, thank the witness for their time, and document the termination in your workplace incident investigator's interview statement. This can occur in both formal investigations and more informal, learning-focused approaches. Even in psychologically safe environments, unresolved tension, fear of blame, or trauma can surface. Maintaining composure and curiosity helps sustain the integrity of the process

If the witness begins ranting abusively, remain calm by breathing deeply and avoiding direct eye contact. Do not allow their words to disrupt your composure. When they seem to have finished, ask, "Is that everything you wanted to say?" If they continue, let them, and then ask again when they appear to have stopped. Eventually, they will run out of things to say, especially if their rant is not having the desired effect on you.

If the witness becomes insulting or abusive, remain calm. Consider asking them to clarify their comments, stating that accurate notetaking is required. The act of repeating an insult often takes the sting out of it. The witness may derive less satisfaction from the insult, which may lead them to stop.

When faced with hostility, having disarming comments ready can help redirect the conversation towards constructive dialogue. For example: "It seems like you have a reason for saying that." Develop your own variations of this statement and memorise them for use when needed. By showing that you are actively listening, the hostility will often reduce.

By carefully managing your approach, body language, and (spoken) language during interviews, you can foster an environment where witnesses feel comfortable and are more likely to provide accurate and valuable information, even in challenging situations.

15 | Witness Interviews — Questioning Techniques

Many workplace incident investigation training programs provide only basic guidance on conducting witness interviews, typically limiting instruction to avoiding closed or leading questions and focusing solely on asking open-ended questions. While this approach is useful, it does not reflect the full range of questioning techniques available to workplace incident investigators. Effective witness interviews require structured, strategic questioning that goes beyond simply avoiding leading questions to elicit accurate and reliable evidence.

Witness evidence is often the most crucial form of evidence in an investigation, making it imperative for workplace incident investigators to develop, refine, and continuously test their questioning techniques. Mastering these skills enables investigators to handle conflicting accounts, assess witness reliability, and gather essential information. This chapter explores a variety of questioning techniques that can be practiced and refined to enhance the quality and integrity of workplace safety investigations. These questioning techniques are valuable across all types of investigations—from formal legal inquiries to learning-focused approaches like learning teams—where the goal is to understand how work is done, not just whether rules were broken.

When conducting witness interviews during a workplace incident investigation, the way you frame your questions is crucial to gathering accurate and comprehensive information. Effective use of questioning techniques to ensure that the witness's account is as clear and detailed as possible, allowing you to piece together the events leading to the incident.

Crafting Questions

All your questions should aim to be:

1. Short and Focused: Each question should be limited to one point or concept. Long, complex questions can confuse the witness and should be avoided.

2. Simple, Plain English: Use straightforward language that is easy for the witness to understand.

3. Polite and Non-Judgemental: Your questions should be polite and non-confrontational to put the witness at ease.

4. Relevant: Use your best judgement to determine the relevance of each question, keeping in mind that the relevance of evidence is not always immediately apparent.

Start the interview with open questions. Open questions are those that cannot be answered with a simple "yes" or "no" and instead invite the witness to provide a narrative response. This style of questioning supports deeper learning and participation, consistent with approaches like learning teams that seek to understand work complexity through open dialogue. For example:

- "Tell me what happened that day."
- "Can you walk me through the events that took place?"
- "How did you come to be involved in this situation?"
- "What would you like to share with me about the incident?"
- "Where would you like to start?"

Encouraging the Witness's Narrative

Allow the witness to tell their story in their own words. Their choice of words, grammar, and overall manner of speaking can provide insight into their state of mind and reliability. As the witness speaks, take notes, organising the information chronologically. Do not hesitate to pause the witness to clarify certain points, ask specific questions, or fill in gaps in the chronology.

For instance:

Workplace incident investigator: "Tell me what happened that day."

Witness: "I arrived on site at 0700 hrs, attended the pre-start, and then went to the third floor to finish the skirting boards in the hallway."

Workplace incident investigator: "Did you go straight to the pre-start when you arrived?"

Witness: "Yes."

Workplace incident investigator: "So, the pre-start started at 0700 hrs or very shortly after?"

Witness: "No, the pre-start started at 0715 hrs."

Workplace incident investigator: "Okay, so what did you do between 0700 hrs and 0715 hrs?"

Using Closed Questions

Closed questions are questions that invite a one-word to answer and should be used sparingly. Overusing them can make the interview feel more like an interrogation, which can make the witness uncomfortable. Closed questions are useful for clarifying specific details, typically at the end of the interview.

Use closed questions:

- To fill a gap in the chronology.

- To verify specific details and assess the witness's reliability.

- To obtain a precise answer when an open question is not yielding the needed information.

- To clarify information or achieve a specific outcome from the questioning.

A closed question should address a single issue and be concise.

Inviting Conclusions

Asking a witness for their opinion or conclusion, such as "What do you think happened?" is generally low-value evidence because it invites speculation rather than focusing on what the witness experienced directly. However, inviting conclusions can be useful when obtaining evidence from expert witnesses who are providing professional judgements based on their expertise.

Testing Witness Reliability

Witnesses may be unreliable due to memory lapses, deception, or bias. One technique to test reliability is to generate a series of questions that solicit very detailed, verifiable information. For example, you want to know if the witness was in the same office room in question. You have a doubt they were in the same one and suspect the witness's recollection is not accurate. You ask:

- "What colour was the chair?"

...but do not stop at one question. It is a series of questions, so continue:

- "What was the chair made from?"
- "Where was the chair positioned?"
- "What were the chair legs made from?"
- "Was there anything on the chair?"
- "Was the base of the chair a different colour?"
- "Were there other chairs in the room that were the same?"
- "Where were the chairs positioned?"

If the witness is truthful, they will either provide accurate information or admit when they do not know the answer. If the witness is attempting to mislead—intentionally or unintentionally—they might fabricate answers that can later be verified.

One Question Too Many

It's important to avoid asking one question too many when the conclusion or inference can already be drawn from what the witness has already said. You do not need the witness to agree with your findings or conclusions – and you do not need to catch the witness lying; document your observations and outline your conclusions in your post-interview statement. Contradictory evidence does not necessarily indicate dishonesty; it may reflect memory gaps.

Presenting the Opportunity for Admission

Sometimes, directly asking a question can make a witness defensive. To avoid this, you can rephrase your questions from inviting a conclusion or admission to one that invites a recollection. For example:

Direct Question: "Did you give way to the oncoming vehicle?"

Rephrased Question: "Did you see the vehicle moving towards you before you pulled out at the intersection?"

The second question is less confrontational and still allows you to infer the necessary information.

Closing Gaps in the Narrative

This more aggressive technique is best used at the end of an interview when you need to drill down on a particular issue. This technique involves asking questions designed to rule out all possibilities except the conclusion you are drawing. However, this approach can make the witness defensive, so it should be used cautiously.

In this example, the workplace incident investigator suspects the emergency exit was blocked by ply board placed there by the witness:

Workplace incident investigator: "Did you leave the ply board in front of the emergency exit?"

Witness: "No."

Workplace incident investigator: "Were you carrying the plyboard?"

Witness: "Yes."

Workplace incident investigator: "Was anyone helping you?"

Witness: "No."

Workplace incident investigator: "Did anyone else move the ply board before the emergency alarm sounded?"

Witness: "No."

In this exchange, the workplace incident investigator methodically rules out any possibility other than the witness leaving the ply board in front of the emergency exit.

Desire for Correction

People often have a strong desire to correct misinformation. By deliberately stating an incorrect fact, you can prompt the witness to provide the correct information, revealing what you need to know.

An employee involved in a forklift incident is being interviewed. The investigator needs to determine whether a medical condition may have contributed to the incident. However, medical history is private information, and the investigator must be cautious about how they approach the question.

Scenario:

The investigator suspects the worker may have a medical condition that could have affected their ability to operate a forklift safely. Rather than directly inquiring about their medical history, the investigator carefully frames the question to maintain privacy.

Exchange:

Investigator: "You have diabetes, but I don't believe this affected your ability to operate safely."

Witness: "No I don't have diabetes; I have sleep apnoea. I have never had diabetes."

Investigator: "I see. Sorry about that, it must be an error."

Seek Outcomes, Not Just Answers

Understanding the outcomes you seek is more helpful than simply framing questions at the outset. For example, instead of asking, "Was a pre-start checklist completed before the forklift was operated?" consider what you need to know: 'I want to understand everything that happened from the operator starting their shift to using the forklift. This will help determine whether a pre-start checklist was conducted.' Now consider what questions would you ask to solicit that information freely from the witness. If you know the outcome, the appropriate questions will naturally follow.

Prioritise Active Listening over Interrogation

The best workplace incident investigator's often ask fewer questions; they focus on listening rather than questioning. Sometimes, simply saying "Tell me what happened" can yield the most valuable information.

Addressing Other Areas of Law and Enquiry

Workplace incident investigations may involve multiple areas of law, and not just health and safety related matters. It may be important to tailor your questions to extract information relevant to other applicable legislation or common law. While you do not need to ask these exact questions, the answers to these questions should emerge from your line of questioning. The answers to these questions are the outcomes being sought:

- Did the person involved breach any organisational policies or procedures?

- Was the person under the influence of drugs or alcohol, or is this suspected?

- Did the person use all required personal protective equipment?

- Has the job been done effectively in the past by this person or others?

- Did the person knowingly engage in a high-risk activity?

- Did the person act illegally?

- How do we know the processes were fit and proper?

- What evidence do we have that people were trained?

- Did the person take steps to avoid the incident?

- Were there signs or warnings about the risks associated with the activity? (This could serve as a final or conclusive question).

It is important to remember that these questioning techniques are not about catching someone out—they are tools to evaluate memory reliability and promote understanding, whether the goal is regulatory compliance, or organisational learning. They should be used to evaluate the reliability of a witness's recollection. These questioning techniques take practice but can enhance witness interviews and provide more reliable evidence for causation analysis.

16 | Expert Witnesses

Expert witnesses can be invaluable to a workplace incident investigator, yet they are seldom utilised in such investigations. An expert witness is typically defined in legislation governing court processes and procedures as:

> "...a person whose opinion, by virtue of education, training, certification, skills, or experience, is accepted by the judge as an expert. The judge may consider the witness's specialized (scientific, technical, or other) opinion about evidence or facts before the court, within the expert's area of expertise, to be referred to as an 'expert opinion.' Expert witnesses may also deliver 'expert evidence' within the area of their expertise. Their testimony may be rebutted by testimony from other experts or by other evidence or facts."[22]

For the purposes of a workplace incident investigation, an expert witness is an individual with specialised knowledge and experience in a particular work process or method, gained through competence and professional expertise. They are uniquely qualified to assess how tasks should be performed and to identify common challenges, risks, or deviations that may occur in practice. They are often another worker within the organisation. Expert witnesses are not only useful in formal or legalistic investigations—they are equally valuable in learning-focused or systems-based approaches, where their insights into practical work realities can enhance organisational understanding.

---

[22] *High Court Rules* 2006 (NZ) rules 9.36-9.46

Why Use Expert Witnesses in Safety Investigations?

In most common law jurisdictions, the legal standard for determining compliance with health and safety duties is based on what is "reasonably practicable." This is an objective test, asking whether a reasonable person in the defendant's position would have taken the same actions. In the context of a safety investigation, the "defendant" could be the organisation, an individual witness, or both. It is critical to determine whether a reasonable organisation or witness in the same position would have acted similarly.

The 'reasonable person' test must account for any specialist knowledge the organisation or witness possesses, making expert witnesses essential. This is where the role of an expert witness becomes essential. An expert witness provides insight into what a competent professional in the same field would have done under similar circumstances at the time of the incident.

An expert witness enables the workplace incident investigator to make informed determinations, such as:

- Whether a procedure was incorrect, incomplete, or otherwise unsuitable (in the incident's circumstances or more broadly).

- Whether the incident was a one-time deviation or indicative of a broader system failure.

- Whether the training provided was ineffective.

For example, if a carpenter used a circular saw to make a specific cut, the expert witness would assess the situation based on the prevailing industry practices and knowledge at the time. They would provide an expert opinion on how that cut should have been performed safely, thereby helping to determine if the carpenter's actions were reasonable.

In another sense, an expert witness's evidence also offers valuable insight into "normal work" or "work as done." They can help determine whether the incident being investigated was a common occurrence or whether it was unique. This insight aligns strongly with contemporary approaches to incident analysis, which focus on understanding how work is actually performed rather than how it is imagined in procedures.

Selecting an Expert Witness

Choosing the right expert witness is a critical step in the investigation and should be approached with care. An expert witness should meet the following criteria:

- Familiarity with Work Processes: They should be well-versed in the relevant work processes and functions, understanding what "normal work" looks like in that context. Their evidence should be confined to their area of expertise.

- Qualifications: They should be suitably qualified, experienced, or both, and their credentials should be documented in the investigation report.

- Impartiality: Ideally, they should have no prior involvement with the incident or those involved.

- Lack of Prior Knowledge of the Incident: They should not be familiar with the specific incident under investigation.

Interviewing an Expert Witness

When interviewing an expert witness, the following approach is recommended (in order):

1. Establish Qualifications: Begin by having the expert witness outline their qualifications, experience, and other criteria that qualify them as an expert.

2. Ask for General Practices: Without revealing the specifics of the incident, ask the expert to describe how they would typically approach or perform the task in question. For example, "How would you go about ripping a piece of timber 1200mm long?"

3. Inquire About Common Pitfalls: Once you have a detailed answer, ask whether there are any common errors or pitfalls that should be avoided with the task in question.

4. Present the Incident Circumstances: Then, present the circumstances of the incident—without naming the individuals involved—and ask whether there is any situation in which it would be appropriate to perform the task in that manner.

5. Ask if they are aware of similar incidents: Find out from them if they are aware of previous, similar incidents or incidents involving the same task.

6. Ask for Their Approach Given the Incident Context: Finally, ask the expert how they would have performed the task under the specific circumstances of the incident.

Asking the questions that relate to these outcomes, in order, will help to indicate what a 'reasonable person' would or should have done in similar circumstances. This reasonable person (objective) test can then be used to help the organisation understand if they are doing everything 'reasonably practicable'.

Steps to Take After Interviewing an Expert Witness

Once the interview with the expert witness is complete, it is important to take the following steps:

- Cross-Check Qualifications and Credibility: Verify the expert's qualifications and credibility. This is crucial, as discovering later that their credentials are not as reliable as initially believed could undermine the weight of their evidence and the overall findings of the investigation.

- Write an Investigator's Statement: Prepare a statement summarising the interview with the expert witness. This statement should outline the claimed credentials, include verifications, and the workplace incident investigator's assessment of the reliability of the witness based on the interview. This assessment will help determine the weight of their evidence in the final report.

- Consider Additional Expert Opinions: Depending on the scale of the investigation and the circumstances of the incident, you may need to seek the opinion of another expert witness. If multiple experts provide consistent evidence, their input should carry significant weight in the findings.

By carefully selecting and interviewing expert witnesses, a workplace incident investigator can gain critical insights that enhance the accuracy and effectiveness of the investigation. Expert witnesses can help to clarify complex technical issues and provide an objective benchmark against which to measure the actions of those involved in the incident. They may also help determine whether the incident was an isolated deviation from an otherwise effective system of work or indicative of a systemic failure within the organisation. Whether the investigation is aimed at legal compliance, system improvement, or team-based learning, expert witnesses help bridge the gap between formal systems and real-world practice.

17 | Other Evidence

In workplace incident investigations, a wealth of information is available regarding the types of evidence a workplace incident investigator can collect. The scale and nature of the incident often dictate what specific evidence is relevant, which can vary significantly between incidents. Therefore, rather than providing a comprehensive list of evidence, this chapter offers insights into types of evidence that have proven useful in the author's experience.

Confidential and Private Information

A workplace incident investigator should determine whether obtaining confidential or private information is necessary. Confidential information might include details about organisational processes, structures, policies, maintenance schedules, or performance records. Private records pertain to individuals and may include recruitment information, employment records, medical information, and curriculum vitae (CVs) or résumés. Access to these types of documents is governed by privacy laws and organisational privacy policies. A workplace incident investigator should be well-versed in the privacy laws applicable in their jurisdiction.

The final investigation report should include notes or a list of evidence that the workplace incident investigator could not obtain, along with the reasons why (e.g., witness refusal, lack of access, budget constraints, or privacy restrictions).

Point-in-Time Documents

Documents are frequently updated; therefore, it is essential to obtain the versions available to individuals at the time of the incident. Regularly updated documents that may be relevant include:

- Organisational procedures and policies.

- Safety Data Sheets for hazardous substances.

- Manuals, including operator's manuals and instructions.

- Field guides.

- Best practice guidelines and good practice guidelines.

- Standards and industry guidelines.

- Plans and drawings.

- Employment contracts and job descriptions.

Equipment Involved in the Incident

The equipment referred to in this section does not include the standard investigation kit a workplace incident investigator typically uses at the start of an investigation. Instead, it refers to the materials and equipment directly involved in the incident.

For any equipment or materials involved in an incident, it is important to gather the following information:

- Size and Dimensions: Documenting the equipment's physical properties.

- Weight: Knowing the weight can be critical in understanding the mechanics of the incident.

- Make, Model, and Date of Manufacture Information: Identifying the specific equipment used.

- Photographs of Equipment Condition: Capturing its state at the time of the incident.

- Guarding: Assessing whether appropriate safety guards were in place. This may require input from an expert witness.

- Service Records: Reviewing the maintenance history of the equipment.

- Operator's Manual: Referring to the manufacturer's guidelines for proper use.

- Functional Checks: Determining whether components like the dead-man switch were defective, the length of time it takes to power down, and what the equipment's capacity was.

Specialist Information

The incident circumstances might make it relevant to engage a specialist to perform data collection or analysis or both. Examples may include sending a contaminated food sample to a laboratory; obtaining a drug and alcohol test for one of the witnesses; or performing air quality sampling. In addition to contributing technical findings, specialist information may offer deeper insights into the conditions of normal work or organisational drift. In learning-oriented investigations, this can support richer understanding and learning, rather than focusing solely on blame or breach.

A workplace incident investigation requires a systematic approach to evidence collection, tailored to the incident's specific nature. Each piece of evidence helps build a comprehensive picture of the incident. Equally important is understanding the boundaries set by privacy laws and recognising when expert or specialist input is required.

18 | Photographs

In the transport industry, specifically in general freight haulage, trucks (called 'road trains') were regularly loaded with a variety of palletised and non-palletised freight and sent across the country, often to remote towns and work sites. Occasionally, load restraint incidents occurred, where inadequately secured freight would fall off a truck. These incidents were often triggered by the increased forces of harsh braking or sharp turns.

When such an incident was reported, it typically came with a series of photographs—close-ups of the fallen freight, images from various angles, and pictures of the damage to the road surface. While these photographs were helpful, they only told part of the story. Often, key aspects were missing from the photographic evidence:

- *There were no photographs of the restraints that had failed or those that had been used.*

- *No photographs captured the truck and trailer as a whole.*

- *Photographs of the road leading into the turn or the skid marks left by the braking truck were absent, which could have provided insight into the direction in which the freight fell, and the forces exerted on it.*

- *Most critically, there were no photographs of the other freight that had remained securely on the truck.*

The absence of photographs showing the freight that stayed secure was a significant oversight. This freight had been subjected to the same forces as the fallen freight but had remained in place due to its restraints. Understanding why this freight stayed secure was essential for determining what would have constituted adequate restraint for the freight that fell.

When conducting workplace incident investigations, capturing accurate and comprehensive photographic evidence is crucial. It is important that photographs taken during investigations include critical details, such as images of restraints, vehicles, and surrounding conditions, as these help in understanding the circumstances of the incident. The use of photographic techniques, including capturing the full context and documenting what went right as well as what went wrong, can strengthen investigations and lead to more effective outcomes.

To ensure that your photographic evidence is as comprehensive and useful as possible, consider the following tips:

- Photographs: Capture images of all relevant details—the individuals involved, witnesses, and the entire scene. A common mistake is failing to capture wide-angle shots of the entire scene. Stepping back and using a wide-angle lens ensures a more comprehensive context.

- Use a Perspective Reference Object: Include a reference object, such as a coin or ruler, in your photographs to provide a sense of scale. This should be a standard item in an investigation kit. For larger perspectives, use a vehicle or a commonly available piece of equipment.

- Recreate the Scene: Recreate the incident scene where safe to do so, ensuring no additional risk is introduced. Use the same personal protective equipment, clothing, time of day, position, and equipment.

- Capture True Colours: If the scene contains substances prone to degradation or oxidation, it is important to capture colour-accurate photographs as close to the time of the incident as possible. However, cameras do not always capture true colours, and each camera will capture colour differently. A colour calibration card (sometimes called a colour passport) can be used to ensure colour accuracy in post-processing.

- Photograph What Went Right: Do not focus solely on what went wrong. It's equally important to take photographs of things that went right under the same circumstances. Understanding why things didn't go wrong under the same conditions can offer valuable insight into system resilience and adaptive capacity. For example:

- If you're investigating a spill or release, take photographs of the containers that did not spill but were in the same area.

- In collision investigations, photograph the positions of nearby vehicles or mobile plant that did not collide. Consider why their outcomes were different.

- For dropped object incidents, capture images of the objects that did not fall.

Technical Specifications for Photographs

If you're confident in your ability to adjust camera settings, here are some technical specifications to aim for:

- Depth of Field: Use a broad depth of field with an aperture of f8 or smaller. This ensures that more of the scene is in focus A large aperture, such as f2.8, will excessively blur the foreground and background, potentially obscuring useful details.

- Focus: A single point focus is usually best, particularly since your subject is likely to be stationary.

- Shutter Speed: A fast shutter speed of 1/60th of a second or faster will be sufficient with a steady hand. If the light conditions do not allow this shutter speed (or a faster shutter speed), use a tripod to avoid camera shake. In low-light conditions, a tripod is essential.

- Avoid Using Flash: Flash can distort colour accuracy and alter lighting conditions, so it should be avoided where possible.

- ISO Settings: Adjust your ISO to fit the aperture and shutter speed settings mentioned above. Low ISO is preferred.

- Lens: A wide-angle lens is essential. Aim for a lens focal length between 15mm and 50mm.

- Test Shot: Capture a test shot with a colour calibration card to verify accurate colour representation.

Depending on the environment, an intrinsically safe camera may be required.

If resources allow, the workplace incident investigator can use an action video camera attached to their helmet or torso to record footage while walking around (there may be privacy implications for this in some jurisdictions). This can provide a valuable reference if the scene needs to be revisited but has changed, or the scene is no longer accessible.

Following these guidelines ensures thorough and effective photographic documentation, providing a complete picture of the incident. This not only helps in understanding what went wrong but also offers insights into what was done correctly.

Part 3
Data Consolidation

19 | Timeline of Events

In any workplace incident investigation, the evidence gathered from various sources—such as photographs, manuals, guides, and witness statements—needs to be meticulously organised and referenced. The document created by the workplace incident investigator from this organised information is known as the Timeline of Events. This structured timeline is equally useful in systems-focused investigations such as learning teams, where the goal is to understand how work unfolds in real conditions and what influenced people's actions over time.

The Timeline of Events should include the following key elements:

- The Date of the Event (if available): The date should be sourced directly from the documents, such as the date a photo was taken, the date a procedure was published, or the date an induction was conducted. Sometimes, the exact date may not be clear, such as when a document is undated, or a witness cannot recall precisely when something happened. In these cases, enter the event on the Timeline of Events on the day(s) you believe it most likely occurred, and mark the date as "not yet known" or leave it blank. As more evidence is gathered, you may be able to narrow down or confirm the date. The date should be recorded in a standard format, such as DD/MM/YYYY.

- The Time of the Event (if available): The time of the event should be recorded if known. In the early stages of creating the Timeline of Events, exact times may not be available, but as the investigation progresses, more precise times will become relevant, particularly as you approach the incident and its aftermath. Record the time to the minute, or to the second if relevant. Use the 24-hour format to avoid any potential ambiguities. If international time zones are relevant, consider adding extra columns to reflect them.

- A Brief Description of the Event: An event is any action that is known or believed to have occurred. This can also be an event that should have happened but didn't, such as an induction that was not conducted when a person started at a particular job, where an induction would normally be required. Each separate action should be recorded as a new entry in the Timeline of Events. Providing detailed descriptions of each event saves time later in the investigation. For instance, if a document was drafted, reviewed, and published on different days, each of these actions should be entered separately on the Timeline of Events. When the event involves a document, such as an email or text message, record the actual text or the relevant portion. This level of detail will be useful in the later stages of the investigation.

- The Evidential Reference for the Event: This is the source of the event, the evidence on which you rely to record the event. The reference should include the name of the evidence source, such as a witness statement, photograph, or operator's manual. Each event in the Timeline of Events must have a verifiable reference. In cases where a single event has multiple references, include all of them to strengthen the validity of the event and the weighting of the evidence that supports it.

Example of a Timeline of Events

The Timeline of Events can be structured as a simple table, like the example below:

Date	Time	Even	Reference
DD/MM/YYYY	10:03 GMT	Example event	Statement of example witness

While it may be tempting to append numerous notes to the Timeline of Events, this should be kept to a minimum and done only if necessary for understanding. If there is something relevant that needs to be noted, it should ideally be based on evidence and integrated into an event entry. If necessary, the event may need to be re-drafted to include this information.

Recording Events from Witness Statements

Witness statements are a key source of evidence and should form a significant part of the Timeline of Events. When recording events from these statements, consider the following guidelines:

- Avoid Speculation: Do not include speculation or surmising from witnesses. This type of information might be relevant for your own statement about the interview or for an expert witness, but it does not belong in the Timeline of Events.

- Focus on Sensory Details: Include only what the witness directly experienced—what they saw, smelled, heard, felt, etc.

- Address Discrepancies: If there are discrepancies between statements from different witnesses, enter both versions of the events and highlight the inconsistencies. The workplace incident investigator's own statement will help to weigh one version against the other. These discrepancies may offer valuable insights into different perspectives and conditions at the time of the event. In a collaborative or systems-based investigation, this variation can help reveal adaptive behaviours or procedural drift that merit further exploration—not just differences in credibility.

- Confidential Information: Mark any private or confidential information accordingly as 'private' or 'confidential.'

- Use Correct Names: Ensure that full names are used, spelled correctly, and linked to any relevant nicknames if applicable.

- Plain Language: Use clear and precise language when recording events, as outlined in the chapter on Confining the Incident.

- Record Facts, Not Conclusions: The Timeline of Events should focus on facts rather than conclusions or outcomes. For example:

- ○ Not Preferred: "The witness's induction was too short."

- ○ Preferred: "The witness's induction duration was 12 minutes."

- ○ Not Preferred: "The witness and the involved person argued."

- ○ Preferred: "The witness and the involved person had a conversation in which they did not agree. Their words to each other were interpreted as heated and aggressive."

- ○ Not Preferred: "The witness saw the involved person go to inspect the crane."

- ○ Preferred: "The witness saw the involved person move toward the crane."

- ○ Not Preferred: "The audit was improperly conducted."

- ○ Preferred: "The witness conducted an audit. The audit covered the following..."

A well-organised Timeline of Events ensures a clear, detailed record essential to the investigation. This methodical approach ensures that all relevant information is accounted for, discrepancies are highlighted, and the facts are presented in a structured manner, contributing to a thorough and accurate investigation. It also helps identify gaps in the evidence, enabling the workplace incident investigator to conduct further enquiries.

20 | Further evidence

Chester Porter was junior counsel to Shand KC in the 1951 Royal Commission into the conviction of Frederick Lincoln McDermott. In 1947 Mr McDermott was convicted of a murder which had happened more than 10 years before... The murderer had driven a car to the scene and the tyre tracks were fresh. Chester Porter tracked down the ancient model of a car similar to Mr McDermott's. It was a 1926 Essex Tourer. He measured the tyre tracks. They did not match the tracks at the scene. The Royal Commission found that the conviction was wrong and Mr McDermott was released.[23]

Invariably, a workplace incident investigator will need to obtain further evidence. This becomes necessary as the workplace incident investigator gains a clearer understanding of what additional information is needed and what can be achieved through re-enactment, additional witness interviews, or further observation. This may not only help identify causes or breaches, but also deepen understanding of how work was actually done at the time of the incident—valuable for both traditional investigations and learning-oriented approaches.

Typically, when a workplace incident investigator first attends the scene, several hours or even days may have passed since the incident occurred. By this time, certain details may have changed or become obscured.

Revisiting the Incident Scene

It is particularly important to make a point of going back to the scene on the same day and at the same time as the incident. While this may not always

---

[23] Ross, David (2007) *Advocacy* Cambridge, Cambridge University Press, paragraph 2120.

yield new information, any insights gained can be invaluable. For instance, you might discover relevant factors that were not previously considered, such as the position of the sun and available lighting, ambient noise levels at that time of day, traffic congestion, or other environmental conditions.

During this revisit, consider using monitoring devices to take environmental readings at the incident scene. Depending on the nature of the incident, you might use a wet bulb thermometer to measure temperature, a lux meter to gauge light levels, a noise monitoring device, or an air monitoring device. Additionally, it could be useful to take similar readings at a comparable location where no incident occurred to identify any notable differences.

As you revisit the scene, take the opportunity to observe other, similar areas where an incident did not occur. Ask: What differs between these areas? What remains the same? What may have changed since the incident? This comparison can help identify factors that contributed to or mitigated the incident in similar contexts. This type of comparative observation supports the identification of variation in "normal work" versus formal procedures or expectations—a key focus in systemic and learning-based investigations.

When revisiting the scene, ensure all measurements are independently verified and rely on primary data whenever possible. This visit is also an opportunity to verify the accuracy of witness statements, particularly if inconsistencies are suspected—such as discrepancies in responses to specific, detailed questions aimed at later verification.

Gathering Additional Information

After conducting initial witness interviews, you will likely identify additional information that needs to be gathered. This might include:

- Conducting further interviews with new witnesses who have come to light.

- Re-interviewing witnesses to clarify details or explore new lines of enquiry.

- Sourcing additional expert witnesses (refer to the chapter on Expert Witnesses).

Organising Evidence

The process of collating and organising evidence is integral to identifying gaps that require further investigation. Using a structured approach such as PEEPO (People, Environment, Equipment, Procedures, and Organisation) or a comprehensive Timeline of Events, workplace incident investigators can ensure no critical aspect is overlooked. For example, reviewing personnel records, environmental conditions, and equipment maintenance logs often reveals factors relevant to causation. Organising evidence provides a comprehensive foundation for investigators to identify missing details and plan subsequent enquiries, enabling a thorough and targeted investigation. This structured approach is equally useful whether the goal is to determine root causes or to support reflective practices that lead to learning and improvement.

By systematically collating and organising evidence and conducting further enquiry—such as revisiting the scene with these considerations in mind—a workplace incident investigator can ensure a thorough investigation without overlooking critical details. This approach not only helps to solidify the findings but also reinforces the reliability and credibility of the investigation's conclusions.

21 | Confining the Incident

Incidents in the workplace can vary in complexity. They may involve just one person or many, result in multiple injuries or none, and may present high levels of potential risk along with various exacerbating factors. Particularly in complex incidents, the chain of causation can easily become conflated, confused, or even unworkable, making it difficult to analyse meaningfully. Consider the following example:

> Imagine a bar fight breaks out between two men. One of the men, armed with a knife, slashes, and stabs the other, ultimately landing a blow to the victim's torso. The victim bleeds profusely, but an ambulance is called, and he is rushed to the hospital. Medical staff determine that the wound is not fatal and, after stopping the bleeding, they expect the victim to make a full recovery. However, during his recovery, the victim's condition rapidly declines. Upon further examination, it is discovered that a contaminated swab was left inside the victim, leading to a severe infection. Due to the infection's proximity to vital organs, the victim dies in the hospital.

Who is responsible for the victim's death?

This scenario raises complex questions about causation:

- Was the stab wound the cause of death? One could argue yes, because the man would not have been in the hospital if not for the stabbing during the fight. But one could also argue no, since the wound itself was not fatal, and the victim was expected to recover fully.

- Was the swab the cause of death? Yes, because the infection resulted from the medical staff's (poor) actions. But again, one could argue no, because the medical procedure would not have been necessary if not for the stab wound that put the victim in the hospital in the first place.

Separating Incidents to Determine Causation

To resolve issues of conflicting or conflating causation in a workplace incident investigation, it is important to separate different incidents within a set of circumstances and consider each as a separate incident requiring its own causation analysis. This approach depends on how the organisation defines an 'incident.' While separated incidents may share the same facts, their causation analyses will differ. Although separated incidents may share the same facts, the causation analysis will take different paths. Where an event in the Timeline of Events is itself an incident, based on your working definition of an incident, then there is a break in the chain of causation because a new incident has intervened. The new incident may rely on the same set of events from the same evidence, but it requires its own causation analysis.

Consider the following definition of an incident: "An event during Company activity, which causes or could have caused an injury, illness, near miss, damage, or privacy breach to personnel (including Contractors, Client staff, the public); plant or equipment; vehicles; property; material; and the environment." Using this definition, consider the following example:

A worker is digging a trench with hand tools while a colleague operates an excavator nearby. The worker in the trench hears a loud buzzing noise. Fearing it is an electrical cable; he scrambles out of the trench and burns his hand on the exhaust of the excavator. Later, it is discovered that there was indeed an electrical cable buried in the area, and it had been damaged, likely by the excavation.

How would you describe this incident?

- Is it an injury (burn to the hand)?

- Is it a near miss (nearly suffered an electric shock)?

- Is it property damage (underground service strike damaging the electrical cable)?

Based on the definition of an incident provided above, the answer is that it is all three, and each of these incidents deserves a separate causation analysis. Each causation analysis will rely on the same evidence from the Timeline of Events. Treating them separately allows for clearer findings and more targeted recommendations.

Determining Multiple Incidents

To determine whether multiple incidents have occurred, it is crucial to examine the facts reported and understand if more than one incident meets the organisation's definition of an "incident." To do this effectively, the information must be accurately interpreted.

Consider the following sentence:

"Emily has three dogs and two cats. They are all brown, but one of the dogs has spots. The dog's name is Spot."

What can we ascertain from this sentence? Which of the following statements are true?

- Emily's cats are brown.

- The cats do not have spots.

- Emily has a male dog.

- Emily owns five pets.

We cannot say with certainty that any of these statements are true. We need more information. Assuming the truth of these statements without evidence is risky and can lead to incorrect conclusions.

Let's look at another example:

"Sam was operating a forklift in the loading dock. There were three pallets in the area, one of which was overhanging the marked zone. The overhanging pallet was struck by the forklift."

Which of the following statements are true?

- The three pallets were in the loading dock.

- Sam was operating the forklift in the marked zone.

- Sam's forklift struck the overhanging pallet.

Again, we cannot say with certainty that any of these statements are true. A workplace incident investigator will need to seek clarity and further information.

English comprehension and accurate wording are essential when starting the investigation analysis. To correctly identify and analyse an incident, you must ask specifically, "What is the incident?" The best approach is to use active sentence structures.

An active sentence follows the word order: subject, verb, object.

Example: John kicked the ball.

- Subject = John

- Verb = kicked

- Object = the ball

A passive sentence reverses this order: object, verb, subject.

Example: The ball was kicked by John.

Passive sentences generally use more words than active sentences, making them harder to understand. In the example, the active sentence contains four words, whereas the passive sentence contains six. Using fewer words improves comprehension. Additionally, passive sentences can sometimes omit the subject entirely:

Example: The ball was kicked.

Such omissions can obscure the actual cause of an incident.

Another word order—object, subject, verb—is rarely used in English and often sounds strange. For instance, Yoda from *Star Wars* often speaks in this order, making his sentences sound peculiar:

Example: The greatest teacher failure is.

Identifying Multiple Incidents

To determine the incident, try to word it as a simple active subject-verb-object sentence. If the sentence is too complex, you likely have multiple incidents within the same set of circumstances, each of which needs to be investigated separately (though they may use the same evidence).

Structuring a sentence in active form makes it easier to determine whether it meets the incident definition.

Consider again the following definition of an incident:

"An event during Company activity, which causes or could have caused an injury, illness, near miss, damage, or privacy breach to personnel (including Contractors, Client staff, the public); plant or equipment; vehicles; property; material; and the environment."

Compare these two actual incident description examples:

"The task was repetitive and strenuous."

"The involved person sprained their elbow."

Which one would you say is an incident?

"The task was repetitive and strenuous" – This is a conclusion, not an incident.

"The involved person sprained their elbow" – This is an incident, as per the definition above.

These examples, taken from the same set of circumstances, highlight the importance of getting the starting point of your analysis correct. Failure to correctly identify the incident risks misanalysing the situation, leading to flawed findings and ineffective recommendations.

An organisation or workplace incident investigator may define 'incident' or 'event' differently. For instance, what one person calls an 'incident' another might call an 'event'. The terms can have many different vernacular meanings, and this is to be expected. A workplace incident investigator should clearly define these terms for the investigation and its final report. Clear definitions and language are critical regardless of the investigation approach used— whether compliance-focused, system-based, or a facilitated learning process. They ensure that all stakeholders interpret findings in a consistent and useful way.

Part 4
Analysis

22 | Investigation Analysis Team

Forming an Investigation Analysis Team is not a common practice in many workplace incident investigations, yet its benefits are significant. Unlike an initial briefing at the start of an investigation—often used in traditional approaches—an Investigation Analysis Team meeting serves a different purpose. Traditional investigations frequently rely on a single investigator or a small team, which can limit perspectives and increase the risk of oversights or bias. In contrast, an Investigation Analysis Team brings together diverse expertise, leading to a more comprehensive review of evidence, better identification of systemic issues, and the development of well-rounded recommendations. This collaborative approach not only enhances the quality and credibility of the investigation but also fosters stakeholder engagement and ensures that findings address both immediate and systemic causes. While it may require additional planning and resources, establishing an Investigation Analysis Team is a proactive and strategic step toward producing meaningful, actionable outcomes. This model is not limited to traditional investigation methods. It aligns well with contemporary learning reviews, human-centric approaches, and systems-thinking models, where the focus is on understanding how work is normally done and how systems can be improved.

Once the Timeline of Events is complete and the incident(s) have been clearly defined, it is crucial to determine who will assist with the causation analysis and form part of the Investigation Analysis Team. This step involves various stakeholders connected to the activity, incident, or process. Including these stakeholders helps to foster engagement and ownership of the findings and recommendations. A thorough analysis requires input from subject matter experts or other relevant stakeholders. The composition and scope of the

Investigation Analysis Team depend on the incident's severity and the investigation's scale. These stakeholders or "relevant persons" may include a combination of the following:

- A worker or worker representative: Someone directly involved in the work or representing the workers' interests. In some jurisdictions it is mandatory to involve elected health and safety representatives in the investigation.

- A senior management representative: This should be someone with the authority to allocate significant resources to any recommendations that might be needed. This may be a company officer, as defined under company law.

- A witness: Carefully consider which witnesses to include. The key witness or injured person may not always be the best choice due to factors like defensiveness or post-incident trauma. If they are not included, consider involving another available witness.

- A subject matter expert: An expert with specific knowledge relevant to the incident or associated processes. This could be an expert witness previously consulted.

- The lead workplace incident investigator: The person responsible for leading the investigation.

- A co-workplace incident investigator or other investigation support person: Additional support to assist with the investigation or another member of the investigation team, if there was more than one person.

- A union representative: If applicable or required under employment law.

In some cases, a single individual might fulfill multiple roles, such as a worker representative who is also a subject matter expert.

Considerations for Legal Professional Privilege (LPP)

It is essential to be mindful of legal professional privilege, which may limit who can be involved in the Investigation Analysis Team. Including unnecessary individuals may risk waiving legal professional privilege; seek legal advice if uncertain. If legal professional privilege must be preserved, obtain legal advice tailored to your circumstances. You may need to pause the investigation pending further instructions from legal counsel to ensure that legal professional privilege is not inadvertently waived.

Role and Purpose of the Investigation Analysis Team

The primary goal of the Investigation Analysis Team is to convene and determine:

- The chain of causation: Identifying the sequence of events that led to the incident, and where it terminates.

- The recommendations: Deciding on recommendations to prevent the incident from recurring.

In some cases, convening an Investigation Analysis Team may be impractical due to the scale of the investigation or severity of the incident. If convening a team is impractical, the lead investigator may conduct the analysis independently. However, seeking input from a subject matter expert or qualified professional for validation is advisable.

Conducting the Investigation Analysis Team Meeting

The meeting should begin with an introduction by the lead workplace incident investigator, covering the following points:

- Goals of the meeting: Clearly state what the meeting aims to achieve.

- Purpose of the investigation: Reiterate why the investigation is being conducted.

- Roles of the Investigation Analysis Team members: Explain why each person is part of the team and what their contributions will be.

- Available evidence: Review the evidence in the Timeline of Events (allowing for a review of the reference for that evidence if needed) that has been gathered and how it will be used in the analysis.

The Investigation Analysis Team Brief

The lead workplace incident investigator should deliver a brief at the start of the meeting that includes:

- Experience with investigation analysis: Ask the team members if they have conducted investigation analysis before.

- Explanation of key terms: Define important terms like "causation", "incident", and "event" to ensure everyone has a common understanding.

- Investigation process overview: Summarise the steps taken so far, including reporting, response, evidence gathering, and the creation of the Timeline of Events.

- Meeting process: Outline how the meeting will proceed, including:

  o Reviewing the Timeline of Events and weighing conflicting evidence.

  o Identifying causative events based on causation analysis tests (see the chapter on Causation Analysis).

  o Determining the causes of those events within the organisation's sphere of influence using deductive logic.

  o Distinguishing between causes that can be directly controlled by the organisation and those that can be influenced by it.

  o Determining recommendations based on the findings.

- Post-meeting actions: Explain what will happen after the meeting, including:

  o Compiling the findings and recommendations, and

○ Developing the final investigation report.

Guiding Principles for the Investigation Analysis Meeting

The lead workplace incident investigator should outline some guiding principles for the meeting. These principles may be subject to the organisation's policies and the investigation's purpose and scope. The following guidelines are typically used:

- Prioritise systemic factors over individual blame: While understanding behaviour and its underlying causes is important, the focus should remain on organisational and procedural improvements - understanding how systems shape behaviour and performance is central to driving meaningful improvement. Consider their actions and behaviours as part of the chain of causation and continue to explore why they behaved in that manner. See the chapter on Behavioural Findings.

- Confidentiality requirements: The lead workplace incident investigator should be familiar with privacy laws and the organisation's confidentiality policies. Discuss how any confidential or private information will be shared and protected.

- Good faith analysis: Emphasise that the team is entrusted with conducting the analysis in good faith.

- Focus on building systemic controls: When considering recommendations, aim to integrate them into the existing system rather than adding bureaucracy, administration, or relying on workers' memory.

- Legal compliance: Consider the legal requirements of the jurisdiction, such as whether the organisation took "all reasonably practicable steps."

- Challenge assumptions: Team members may have already formed ideas about the causes and findings. These assumptions will likely be tested during the meeting, which may be challenging but is an integral part of the process.

A well-structured Investigation Analysis Team meeting significantly enhances the reliability of causation analysis. By following these guidelines, the team can effectively identify the causes of incidents and recommend corrective actions that address these causes, leading to safer workplace practices and environments.

23 | Causation Analysis

At this stage, a comprehensive Timeline of Events should have been developed, with individual incidents identified. Depending on the scale of the investigation, you may have assembled a team of relevant persons to assist in determining causation and analysing the events. Now, it's time to look at the incident (or incidents) based on the definition adopted by your organisation. In other words, there should be a precise point in the timeline where the incident occurs in clear terms. This identified point serves as the starting reference for the causation analysis. This causation analysis model can be applied regardless of your chosen investigation methodology—whether it is a traditional fact-finding model or a contemporary learning-oriented approach. The process is adaptable to suit the purpose of your investigation, whether it is regulatory, organisational learning, or both.

Distinguishing Between the Incident and Events

It is crucial to distinguish between the 'incident' itself and the 'events' leading up to it. An event is any individual entry in the Timeline of Events. Note that an incident may have a causative event that is itself an incident – this would be subject to its own causation analysis (see the Chapter on Confining the Incident). Each event represents a single action—something known or believed to have occurred—rather than an omission or an unfulfilled expectation. It could also include instances where an event should have occurred but didn't (such as a scheduled audit that was not carried out). Distinguishing between an omission that should be excluded (e.g., neglecting to act due to poor judgement) and an event that should have occurred but did not can be challenging. The workplace incident investigator can exercise their judgement, based on the available evidence, to make this distinction. This detailed parsing of events helps provide clarity in both linear investigations and those aiming to understand broader system conditions and adaptive behaviours.

The Chain of Causation

To determine causation, we need to analyse the Timeline of Events in a systematic way. Causation is analysed retrospectively, requiring us to trace events backward from the marked incident. Each event in the Timeline of Events should be assessed using three tests to determine its relevance and causal impact.

The First Test: Necessary Condition

The first test you should apply is the Necessary Condition test. This involves asking whether the event was a necessary condition for the occurrence of the incident. In simpler terms, could the incident have occurred without this event? This is also known as the "but for" test in legal factual causation.

- Counterfactual Analysis: To effectively apply this test, introduce a counterfactual scenario. Consider: If this event had not occurred or had unfolded differently, would the incident still have happened? An expert witness's statement (as defined in this book) and input from a subject matter expert in the Investigation Analysis Team can be invaluable in establishing these points by identifying deviations from expected practices.

    - No: If the answer is no, meaning the incident could not have occurred without this event, then this event is a necessary condition. Add it to your list of causative events.

    - Yes: If the answer is yes, meaning the incident could still have occurred without this event, proceed to the next test.

The Second Test: Presumptive and Proximity Tests

The second test is twofold: the Presumptive Test and the Proximity Test.

1. Presumptive Test: Start by asking whether the event increased the likelihood or severity (or both) of the incident. This test considers events that might have been designed to prevent the incident but failed (such as failed controls), or events that were not a necessary condition yet still contributed to the likelihood or severity. These are termed "presumptive events."

2. Proximity Test: Once an event is identified as a presumptive event, you must then consider its proximity to the incident. Did this presumptive event occur sufficiently close to the incident to be deemed relevant? The concept of proximity is subjective and depends on the incident's nature. It should not be a 'far-fetched or fanciful' connection. It should be reasonably foreseeable.

   - Yes: If the answer is yes, the event is relevant. Add it to your list of causative events.

   - No: If the answer is no, proceed to the third test.

The Third Test: Events as Intended

The third test is to determine whether any events on the Timeline of Events were contrary to what was supposed to happen. This test considers whether any inconsistencies, acts or omissions, or behaviours deviated from the ideal or expected outcomes, regardless of whether they directly contributed to the incident.

- Yes: If the answer is yes, the event is relevant and should be added to your list of causative events.

- No: If the answer is no, the event is not considered a key event.

A statement from an expert witness (as defined in this book) and input from a subject matter expert in the Investigation Analysis Team can be invaluable in identifying deviations from expected procedures.

The following example demonstrates the application of these tests. The Timeline of Events is based on a real incident investigation, with identifying details removed. Also, some events have been removed, where those events are not material to a reader's understanding of the events and not material to the chain of causation.

The Timeline of Events is an example only, for illustrative purposes.

- Necessary conditions are in **bold**.

- Proximal Presumptive events are in *italics*.

- Events as intended are <u>underlined</u>.

- The incident is in CAPITALS.

IP means 'involved person'.

Date	Time	Event	Reference Document
2006 – 2013		Work experience: The involved person (IP) worked with previous construction companies. Inconsistencies noted in documents given to recruitment, such as: Résumé states employed with – • Building Company 1 2011- 2013 (2 years employment) and • Building Company 2 in 2013 A personal reference from Building Company 1 states: • IP's employment lasted approx. 4 years through to June 2014	IP's Resume and personal references
1/8/14		The IP attends urine drug test in Canada. Negative result	Drug Test Results
29/08/14		The IP arrived in the country	IP's statement
30/08/14		The IP attended a company induction at Employer's Office	IP's statement
01/09/14		Client 1 site. The IP was on site for approx. 1.5 weeks. • Cedar laminating, underneath canopy • Operated skill saw and various other saws	IP's statement
05/09/14		The IP attended Client 2 site	IP's statement
02/09/14 & 09/09/14		Saturdays - Also worked at Client 2 site • Framing windows for fitting, fitted windows, wall to be framed up ready for cement boards. • Above task required plastic battens and wooden battens to be cut to size	IP's statement
02/09/14		The IP attended a site induction with Witness 1. The IP cannot recall if paperwork was completed. No paperwork on file.	IP's statement

Date	Time	Event	Reference Document
10/09/14		Witness 1 was inducted to site by Witness 2 and was not on-site at Client 2 site consistently. Witness 1 on site for a 2-week period. Saturday works. The IP was working at the Client 1 site.	Witness 1 statement
12/09/14		The IP's induction form completed by Witness 1 but not signed by IP	Induction form dated 12/9/17
12/09/14 – 14/09/14	0630	Witness 1 began installing windows (after removing the old ones) and framing around them. The previous week, a wall had been framed, and this week, the IP was completing it. IP was doing a job connected with a part of the wall. During the week IP built a windowsill, installed windows – framing work. IP was helping with screwing in pieces of timber using a rotary hammer drill.	Witness 1 statement
12/09/14		1. A Task Analysis developed for Window Demolition. Plant required: Hand tools and circular saw • The IP did not sign the task analysis 2. Task Analysis developed for reinstating windows. Plant required: Nail guns, rotary hammer drill, stapler, and hand tools. The IP did not sign the task analysis	Task Analysis Worksheets dated 14/6/17

Date	Time	Event	Reference Document
13/09/14		Task Analysis developed for rendering concrete. Plant required: scaffolding, trowels, and cement. • No sign off by IP 3. Task Analysis did not cover use of circular saw	Task Analysis Worksheet dated 15/6/17
13/09/14	0630 – 1630	The IP was on shift at Client 2 site	Supervisor's notes
13/09/14		IP attended an on-site meeting delivered by Witness 1. Topics discussed included: • Importance of wearing PPE when using power tools • Attitude • Smoking • Mobile Phones • Housekeeping • Other contractors and small spaces • Dust and fire alarms	Signed onto Meeting minutes dated 13/9/17
14/09/14		The IP was advised to put his earplugs back in by Witness 1. The IP said in this instance, "They are my ears; I can do what I like with them'. The IP may have said this often during his time with the company.	Witness 1 statement - **hearsay**

Date	Time	Event	Reference Document
15/09/14	0630	• The IP commenced their shift at Client 2 site • The IP conducted informal pre-start re job sequence for the job. Finishing work from the previous day. Framing out walls with battens and building wrap. The IP used tin snips to cut plastic to size. The IP would have used a saw to cut various pieces of timber several times.	Supervisor's notes and IP's statement
	0630 - 0830	The IP was asked by Witness 1 to arrange plastic battens and attach them to the wall with a hammer (no need to saw) and to remove leftover pieces of scaffolding from the ground floor.	Witness 1 statement
	0830	IP was removing flashing, which was installed incorrectly. Pull out nails and pull of wall.	Witness 1 statement
	0900	Witness 1 left to collect materials from the supplier.	Witness 1 statement
	1000	• Witness 1 returned and sent workers on a break. • Morning tea break 1000-1030 hrs.	Witness 1 statement
	1030	Witness 1 delivered toolbox re Dust Encapsulation for powered cutting tools	IP's statement
	1045-1245	The IP started back at work training wall with plastic battens, timber battens as above	IP's statement and Witness 1' statement

Date	Time	Event	Reference Document
		The IP went to use a table/bench which had two pieces of 12 cm x 5 cm timber protruding on the 'non-wall' edge of the table. **These pieces were not clamped down or secured in any way.**	Photographs 9, 22, 28–30, 34–35, 41–44, and 46–47, 56–57.
		Witness 1 did not instruct the IP to cut timber; the assigned task was to attach battens.	Witness 1 statement
	1246-1250 (time of incident)	As the IP's lunch break was scheduled for 1300 hrs, they attempted to cut a piece of wood beforehand. The cut was a *rip cut to a piece of 12 cm x 5 cm,* which needed to be halved again to fit wall framing.	IP's statement
		The IP placed a 10mm x 60mm x 1500mm timber splinter on the two protruding 2x4 pieces to perform a rip cut with a circular saw. **It was neither clamped nor secured.**	Photographs 9, 28, 22, 26, 29, 30, 34, 35, 43, 44, 47
		The circular saw blade was set to approximately 35mm	Photographs 26, 29, 39,
		The circular saw was a right-handed circular saw. The IP used his left hand to operate the circular saw	Video 1; Photographs 26, 29, 36, 40,
15/09/14		**The IP used his right hand to hold the splinter of timber in place resting on the 2x4 pieces protruding from the table**	Video 1

Date	Time	Event	Reference Document
		The IP cut the timber lengthways in the middle (ripping).	Video 1; Photographs 9, 26, 29, 35, 30, 43, 47
		INCIDENT: THE CIRCULAR SAW BLADE CONTACTED A KNOT IN THE TIMBER, CAUSING THE CIRCULAR SAW TO 'KICK BACK' TOWARDS THE IP, AND IN THE MOTION OF THE CIRCULAR SAW MOVING BACK WITH HIS LEFT HAND, THE MOVING BLADE CONTACTED IP'S RIGHT THUMB.	Video 1
	1247	The IP attended the first aid kit with Witness 1 who administered first aid	IP's statement; photographs 23, 24, 25
	1312	The IP was admitted to hospital.	Medical Record
	1616	The incident responder contacted the workplace safety regulator to seek guidance regarding whether the incident could be considered a reportable injury.	Incident Responder's Statement
17/09/14	1036	The IP was discharged from Hospital. The IP's medical care was transferred to the IP's General Practitioner.	Medical Record
20/09/14		The workplace safety regulator sent a mail confirmation (received on this date) acknowledging notification of the incident.	Regulator Confirmation of Notification Letter dated 20/9/14

From the example Timeline of Events above, the incident and the results of the three causation analysis tests are listed below.

Incident:

The circular saw blade contacted a knot in the timber, causing the saw to 'kick back' toward the involved person (IP). In the motion of pulling the circular saw back with his left hand, the moving blade contacted the IP's right thumb, resulting in injury.

Note: This incident meets the definition of an incident used by the organisation. No other events in the Timeline of Events meet the definition of an incident.

Necessary Conditions:

- The IP used his right hand to hold a splinter of timber in place, resting it on two protruding 2x4 pieces of timber on the table. This piece of timber was not clamped down or secured in any way.

  This is a necessary condition because, had the IP not done this, the incident could not have occurred.

- The IP chose to use a table with two pieces of 2x4 timber protruding from its edge, which was not against a wall. These pieces were neither clamped nor secured.

  This is a necessary condition because, had the IP not done this, the incident could not have occurred.

Presumptive Proximal Events:

- The IP operated the circular saw using his left hand. The circular saw used was designed for right-handed operation.

  This increased the risk of the incident and occurred in close temporal proximity to it.

- The timber being cut measured 12 cm x 5 cm, a size that makes rip cuts difficult and may have contributed to instability during the cutting process.

  This increased the risk of the incident and occurred in close temporal proximity to it.

Events as Intended:

- The IP was not instructed by Witness 1 to cut timber; the assigned task was to install battens.

  This deviates from expected outcomes

- The IP disregarded safety by stating, 'They are my ears; I can do what I like with them'.

  This deviates from expected behaviours.

- The induction form was completed by Witness 1 but was not signed by the IP.

  This deviates from expected procedures.

- During the site induction with Witness 1, it is unclear whether the required paperwork and corresponding processes were completed, as no paperwork is available on file.

  This deviates from expected outcomes.

- A Task Analysis was developed for rendering concrete, including the use of scaffolding, trowels, and cement, but it was not signed off by the IP.

  This deviates from expected procedures.

- A Task Analysis was developed for window demolition, requiring the use of hand tools and a circular saw. The IP did not sign it, possibly indicating it was unread.

  This deviates from expected procedures.

- A Task Analysis was developed for reinstating windows, which included the use of nail guns, a rotary hammer drill, a stapler, and hand tools. The IP did not sign this task analysis either possibly indicating it was unread.

  This deviates from expected procedures.

- A personal reference from Building Company 1 indicates that the IP's employment lasted approximately four years, ending in June 2014, which conflicts with the IP's own résumé.

  This is an unexpected inconsistency.

After applying these three tests, you should have compiled a list of causative events similar to the example above. At this stage, remember that you are not identifying 'the' cause but rather determining whether an event is 'a' cause or a contributing factor to the incident.

The next step in your analysis is to apply deductive logic to each item on the list of causative events you have now identified. This involves systematically examining each event to understand its role in the chain of causation, ensuring that the final conclusions drawn are based on sound reasoning and evidence.

24 | Logic in investigations

In a remote construction site kitchen, a resident reported finding a severely mouldy frankfurter sausage in the lunch packing area. The kitchen staff immediately removed the sausages from service. An investigation began. On inspection, none of the other sausages showed signs of mould, and there were no additional sausages in storage.

The kitchen confirmed that sausages were delivered twice a week and placed out for service immediately, with leftovers used at the next meal. By the third service, sausages were always gone, meaning no leftover sausage could have been mouldy within that time frame.

The mouldy sausage was sent to a lab, where results showed it would take more than a week for mould to grow to the observed level in ideal conditions, far longer than the three days sausages remained in the kitchen. Temperature checks at every stage of storage and transportation confirmed no issues, and staff confirmed the sausages had been handled properly.

This evidence indicated the mouldy sausage could not have come from the kitchen. It must have been brought in or removed and stored improperly before being deliberately placed in the tray to cause a food safety incident. With a multi-million-dollar contract under negotiation at the time, the investigation was able to rule out other findings and infer this was an act of sabotage aimed at damaging the kitchen's reputation.

In the realm of workplace incident investigations, two key skills are indispensable for determining valid causation: English comprehension and logic. While English comprehension helps in accurately interpreting the facts and events surrounding an incident, logic provides the framework for analysing those facts to arrive at sound conclusions. This chapter discusses the application of logic, particularly deductive logic, in the investigation process, and outlines how to use these skills effectively to determine causation.

Valid deductive logic is a critical tool for workplace incident investigators, especially when determining causation. To accurately identify the causes and contributing factors of an incident, workplace incident investigators must construct sound arguments based on reliable evidence while avoiding logical fallacies. There are several benefits to using valid deductive logic.

Avoiding Logical Fallacies: Valid deductive logic helps workplace incident investigators avoid common fallacies, such as the post hoc fallacy, where one assumes that because one event followed another, the first event caused the second. Applying valid logic helps investigators avoid making unfounded causal claims. These principles of reasoning are just as important in learning reviews or "new view" investigations, where understanding how work actually unfolds—and why it made sense at the time—is essential to learning and improvement.

Evaluating Causal Relationships: Deductive logic provides a clear framework for evaluating the strength of causal relationships. Workplace incident investigators can systematically identify possible causes and contributors, and weigh the evidence supporting each one, leading to more informed conclusions.

Identifying Gaps in Evidence: If conflicting reports or missing information exist, deductive logic helps workplace incident investigators identify what additional evidence is needed to construct a sound argument, ensuring a thorough investigation.

Understanding Logic

Logic is a fundamental tool used by philosophers to examine knowledge, reality, and existence, and it is equally critical for workplace incident investigators. Logic involves the use of premises and conclusions that are related to each other in a structured way. Consider the following example of a logical argument:

Premise 1: The forklift's brakes are faulty.

Premise 2: All faulty brakes increase stopping distance.

Conclusion: Therefore, the forklift's stopping distance is increased.

In this argument, the premises lead to a logical conclusion. Our focus is not on the truth of the premises, but on whether the conclusion logically follows from them. In this case, it does: if the premises are true, then the conclusion must also be true. This reasoning process is known as deductive logic.

Here are some more examples of deductive logic:

Valid Argument:

"All forklift operators must complete safety training. Alex is a forklift operator; therefore, Alex must complete safety training."

If the premises are true, the conclusion must be true.

Invalid Argument:

"Some workers did not wear their PPE, and some workers were injured; therefore, some injuries were caused by not wearing PPE."

This argument is invalid because the injured workers may not be the ones who failed to wear PPE.

Valid Argument:

"Either the equipment malfunctioned, or the operator made an error. The equipment did not malfunction; therefore, the operator made an error."

The premises entail the conclusion, although the truth of the premises would need verification.

The key to validating premises is ensuring they are based on evidence. In a workplace incident investigation, each factual statement in the analysis must be supported by evidence. Once the incident is correctly defined and the causative events are identified using simple, active sentences, deductive logic can be applied to analyse them.

Applying Deductive Logic to Causative Events

Causation is fundamentally an application of logic to a sequence of events, often summarised as an 'if-then' relationship:

If X, then Y.

If both X and Y occur, then Z follows.

For example, "If water leaks onto the carpet, and water damages carpets, then the carpet will be damaged."

When analysing the list of causative events, think of them as "then" statements—things that happened. The goal is to identify the "if" statements— what led to them—by asking "why?" This turns the analysis into a "Why? Because..." process, helping to trace the causes step by step. This method applies deductive logic in a practical way to determine causation.

If deductive logic cannot be applied, it is likely because the premises do not support the conclusion. To resolve this issue, you may need to:

- Gather More Evidence: This could involve taking additional witness statements or gathering more physical evidence, such as measurements or photographs.

- Re-examine Existing Evidence: Revisit the evidence you already must see if something was missed or misinterpreted.

Not all investigations will yield a neat, deductively supported conclusion. This is especially true in learning-oriented reviews, where the purpose may be to uncover normal variability, complexity, or adaptation in work—not just determine fault or causation. If deductive logic still cannot be applied, the Investigation Analysis Team (or the investigator if working alone) must use their judgement to determine an outcome, acknowledging that a clear causal connection could not be established in that instance. This is using inference to draw a conclusion and is known as inductive logic.

The Importance of Drawing Inferences

As Bruggink states, "we must not only be able to gather facts but must also be able to draw inferences and deal with assumptions to help place our facts in perspective."[24] This means ruling out any option other than the conclusion you have drawn, even if that conclusion is based on inference rather than direct evidence. For example, consider the Frankfurter Sausage case, where the conclusion was drawn from inference and the ruling out of alternative explanations.

Applying sound logic in workplace incident investigations is essential for determining causation. By grounding your analysis in logic and evidence, you can avoid common pitfalls, evaluate causal relationships, fill gaps in the evidence, and reduce bias. Whether your investigation is aimed at accountability, understanding system behaviour, or driving learning and improvement, grounding your findings in logic and evidence ensures clarity, fairness, and credibility.

---

[24] Ellis, Glenn, *Air Crash Investigation of General Aviation Aircraft,* Capstain Publications, Greybill, WY, 1984, TL553.5 E45 as quoted in Ferry, TS *Modern Accident Investigation and Analysis: Second Edition* (1988) John Wiley and Sons, Inc.

Part 5
Findings, Recommendations
and Reporting

25 | Behavioural Findings

Never attribute to malice or stupidity that which can be explained
by moderately rational individuals following incentives in
a complex system.[25]

A chef working on a remote site starts a 12-hour shift. In the morning, they
burn the webbing between their thumb and index finger on the side of a
hot pan. Despite the pain, they put on gloves and continue working for the
remaining nine hours.

That evening, after removing the glove, they notice a blister. Knowing that
reporting the injury would trigger a lengthy investigation and disciplinary
review under the site's "just culture" policy, they decide to self-manage.
Using nail clippers, they pop the blister and go to bed.

The next day, they oversleep, rush to get ready, and ignore the increasing
discomfort. They put on gloves and work another 12-hour shift. That evening,
the pain worsens, and they suspect an infection but choose to sleep on it.

By the following day, the pain is severe. They visit the on-site medical offi-
cer, who diagnoses a necrotising soft tissue infection requiring immediate
evacuation to a hospital. There is a serious risk of losing their hand.

The incident now escalates to a high-level investigation. The "just culture"
framework is applied, concluding the chef was reckless in self-treating the
injury. The site's management prohibits "reckless" individuals from working
on-site, and the chef is dismissed a week before Christmas.

---

[25] Douglas W. Hubbard (2020) *The Failure of Risk Management: Why it's broken and how to fix*
it, 2nd ed. John Wiley and Sons, Inc.

Discussions about blame, no-blame, and just culture in safety investigations often lead to confusion and the conflation of distinct concepts. To provide clarity, it's important to distinguish between three key areas where these concepts come into play: incident reporting, causation analysis, and the outcomes of investigations. Each area has its own set of considerations and implications, which are explored in this chapter.

Incident Reporting

One of the major deterrents to reporting incidents is the fear of negative consequences. Workers may hesitate to report incidents because they fear:

- Facing disciplinary actions themselves.

- Causing a colleague to face disciplinary actions.

- Delaying work progress or missing targets.

- Being labelled a 'snitch', 'informant' or 'whistleblower'.

- Being subjected to extended reporting and investigation procedures, drug testing, or medical assessments.

Given these potential barriers, implementing a no-blame policy specifically for those who report incidents can be an effective way to encourage reporting. Under a no-blame policy, individuals who report incidents are assured that they will not face adverse disciplinary actions because of their reporting. Those who fail to report incidents may face disciplinary action—not for the incident itself, but for failing to report it. This policy, if followed, can foster a psychologically secure environment where workers can report errors and incidents without fear of the consequences.

Causation Analysis

The concept of no-blame is sometimes misunderstood in the context of causation analysis. It is often mistakenly interpreted as focusing solely on system errors while ignoring poor behaviour. However, the reality is more nuanced. In any investigation, human behaviour is often a relevant factor in the chain of causation. It is important to recognise that while behaviour may be a contributing factor, it should not be the endpoint of the chain of causation inquiry.

When a person's behaviour is identified as relevant, the investigation should delve deeper to understand the underlying causes and contributors of that behaviour. Underlying causes and contributors are numerous and varied, and may include:

- Fatigue: If the individual was fatigued, perhaps the organisation should investigate potential scheduling issues or underlying health concerns.

- Substance Influence: If the individual was under the influence of substances, perhaps the organisation should examine the effectiveness of its drug and alcohol policies.

- Intentional Misconduct: If the behaviour was intentionally harmful, perhaps the organisation should evaluate its hiring and screening processes.

People's behaviour is often influenced by organisational, job, and individual factors.[26] This highlights the importance of continuing the investigation beyond individual actions. Ceasing to explore causation beyond a person's behaviour does little to address the underlying causes or prevent similar actions by others. This is a core principle of "new view" investigations and learning reviews, which emphasise understanding how behaviour made sense to the person at the time, rather than judging it in hindsight.

Outcomes of Investigations

The most contentious aspect of the blame/no-blame debate arises in the context of investigation outcomes, particularly when it comes to disciplinary actions. Views on this topic can be broadly categorised into three perspectives:

---

[26] Health and Safety Executive (1999) *Reducing Error and Influencing Behaviour*, HSG48. HSE Books.

1. Accountability for Reckless Behaviour: This perspective holds that individuals who engage in reckless or intentionally harmful behaviour should be held accountable through disciplinary actions, such as warnings or termination.

2. No-Blame Approach: The opposite perspective argues that no disciplinary consequences should result from an investigation, as this could discourage reporting and hinder learning.

3. Restorative Just Culture: This approach advocates for accountability, but with a focus on supporting individuals through a process of learning and improvement.

It is important to consider the logical implications of concluding an investigation with a focus on an individual's behaviour. Although disciplinary action may be necessary in some cases, it should be carefully balanced to avoid discouraging future incident reporting.

The Concept of Just Culture

Just culture is often invoked in discussions about incident outcomes, but it is a concept that is frequently misunderstood and misapplied. In its essence, just culture seeks to balance accountability with fairness, focusing on learning and improvement rather than punishment. However, this concept can be problematic when it leads to a predetermined search for accountability, regardless of the circumstances.

The use of the term 'just' invokes associations with 'justice'. Necessary for the idea of 'just' and 'justice' are the concepts of a 'victim', a 'perpetrator', and a 'punishment'. Justice-related language is inherently linked to blame and punishment. For this reason, many contemporary learning-focused investigation approaches avoid justice-related terminology altogether, recognising that even well-intentioned language can subtly reinforce punitive mindsets. The concept of 'Restorative Just Culture' still makes these implications, even if the outcomes are less blame oriented. In many safety incidents, the individual involved is both the cause of the incident and the victim. Seeking justice against someone for self-inflicted harm within the context of workplace incidents raises ethical concerns.

Unlike the legal system, which includes due process and procedural fairness, organisational just culture processes often lack these safeguards. If an organisation is going to label a process as 'just', procedural fairness and natural justice should be strictly followed. This is seldom the case in practice and therefore the language of 'just culture' should be reconsidered.

In workplace investigations, concepts such as blame, no-blame, and just culture must be applied thoughtfully and appropriately. By distinguishing between incident reporting, causation analysis, and investigation outcomes, organisations can create a culture that encourages reporting, thoroughly investigates causes and contributors, and promotes learning and improvement.

26 | The End of the Chain of Causation

'Surely the root cause of every event is the Big Bang!' [27]

In workplace incident investigations, determining where to draw the line in the chain of causation is crucial. While tracing the origin of an incident back to the Big Bang is clearly absurd, it highlights the need to establish a practical endpoint in the chain of causation. This is necessarily arbitrary. The challenge lies in knowing where to stop and ensuring that the conclusions drawn are meaningful.

For some, the investigation concludes when a procedural deviation is identified, often aligning with blame-oriented or just culture models. However, these approaches often miss deeper systemic issues and fail to provide meaningful insights that can prevent future incidents. Others may rely on arbitrary decisions influenced by individual or organisational perspectives, which, though reasonable at the time, can be restrictive and inconsistent across incidents.

Some investigation methodologies predefine 'root cause' categories, limiting the scope of investigations. While categorising causes can help in identifying trends, it is not advisable to wait for trends to emerge before addressing issues. If an investigation's purpose is to 'prevent recurrence', then classifying incidents solely to monitor for trends is counterproductive. It can also lead to a situation where the organisation's incident trend record becomes a "database

---

[27] Circus of Safety, *Root Cause Analysis*, 16 December 2023, podcast – accessed on the Overcast app.

of failure," with potential legal implications, particularly if referenced during future regulatory investigations or legal proceedings.

The Organisation's Sphere of Influence and the Chain of Causation

An organisation's sphere of influence includes everything it can affect but not directly control, such as the actions of people and systems it interacts with. Though it may be tempting to conclude the investigation once a cause fits a certain classification, such an approach restricts the depth of causal analysis. The chain of causation should be traced to the edge of the organisation's sphere of influence, where the organisation can still exert some influence, even if not direct control.

An investigation's logical endpoint should lie at the boundary of the organisation's sphere of influence. When formulating recommendations, it is prudent to step slightly back from this boundary. This principle is applicable across investigation methodologies, including traditional, systems-based, and learning-oriented models. Regardless of the approach, defining the endpoint based on influence—not fault—supports more effective recommendations. There are two key reasons for this approach:

1. Indirect Influence: At the edge of the organisation's sphere of influence, the organisation can only effect change indirectly or through influence. Recommendations at this level should aim to leverage that influence effectively.

2. Direct Control: Before reaching the edge of the organisation's sphere of influence, there will be points where the organisation can exert direct control. Recommendations made here should focus on actions that the organisation can implement directly.

Example of Determining the Endpoint of Causation

Consider the following example to illustrate the approach:

- A workplace safety regulator issues an improvement notice to a construction company because workers are removing a manufacturer-supplied guard on a circular table saw to perform specific cuts. According to the regulator's position, if a device includes a manufacturer-supplied guard, it must be used.

- The investigation reveals that the cuts in question can only be performed by removing the guard, as no other tool is suitable. It's also found that the guard supplied by the manufacturer does not meet the applicable machine standard's definition of a machine guard.

From this investigation, several recommendations can be made:

1. Direct Control:

- Issue a directive to all operators to avoid removing the guard unless performing specific cuts where removing the guard is required.

- Develop an alternative process for performing the cuts with the guard removed.

- Perform a risk assessment to manage the cuts safely, in line with industry best practices.

- Explore the development of an alternate custom guarding system that allows the cuts to be performed safely.

2. Indirect Influence:

- Approach the manufacturer to inform them that their guard does not meet the applicable standard and suggest they develop a compliant system.

- Apply pressure on the regulator to reconsider its policy position based on the investigation's findings.

These steps allow the organisation to address both direct and indirect factors within its sphere of influence. These recommendations are more effective than disciplining a worker for not using a guard—an approach found inadequate—or issuing a blanket directive against guard removal.

In any workplace incident investigation, it is essential to understand where to draw the line in the chain of causation. This endpoint should be determined by the limits of the organisation's sphere of influence, instead of a person's behaviour or a predetermined root cause classification. By focusing on both direct control and indirect influence at the edge of the organisation's sphere of influence, organisations can develop more effective strategies to prevent future incidents and avoid some of the pitfalls of blame-oriented approaches.

27 | Recommendations

'Recommendations that follow from an investigation need to be tailored to the organisation and their development needs: there is no 'correct' or absolute set of recommendations that follow from any given incident'[28]

Developing clear and actionable recommendations is a critical skill for any workplace incident investigator, especially for those conducting internal investigations. To ensure recommendations lead to meaningful improvements, they must be well-prioritised, realistically resourced, and precisely worded. These three factors—priority, resourcing, and wording—determine the feasibility, impact, and successful implementation of recommendations. These principles apply across investigation types. Recommendations should be tailored to fit the method used and the learning or compliance outcomes sought by the organisation.

Priority

Determining the priority of a recommendation involves deciding how soon it should be completed. The priority should be based on the proximity of the cause or contributor to the incident within the Timeline of Events. In other words, the closer an event is to the incident on the timeline, the higher the priority it should be given. This approach ensures that the most critical issues are addressed first, potentially preventing a recurrence of the incident. Priority recommendations may become apparent at earlier stages of the investigation, and they should be made known to the organisation as soon

---

[28] Robert J. de Boer in his book *"Safety Leadership - A different, Doable and Directed Approach to Operational Improvement"* highlights the purpose of incident investigations is to distil lesson to prevent reoccurrence.

as possible. In other words, if action can be taken before the investigation concludes, it should be recommended immediately.

Resourcing

Recommendations may also suggest the resources needed for implementation. While this often involves financial resources, it does not necessarily require specifying a dollar amount. Instead, consider the total investment required as 'a percentage of the organisation's available resources available for addressing the outcomes of the investigation'. The workplace incident investigator should recommend the proportion of resources to allocate to each recommendation.

It's important for the workplace incident investigator to ensure that these resource allocations add up to 100%. This approach provides a clear and actionable framework for the organisation to prioritise and allocate resources effectively.

Wording

Clear, specific wording is critical for actionable recommendations. In some cases, the workplace incident investigator may not have enough knowledge of the organisation to recommend systemic changes. In such cases, the recommendation could be to investigate issues further and understand the feasibility of further recommendations.

Developing effective recommendations requires collaboration with several key individuals or stakeholders:

- Subject Matter Expert: This person can confirm whether the recommendation is feasible and desirable.

- Senior Management Representative: This person has the authority to allocate resources and ensure the recommendation is implemented.

- Workplace incident Investigator: Ideally, the lead investigator is skilled in crafting precise and actionable recommendations.

Involving the Investigation Analysis Team helps secure stakeholder buy-in. A poorly crafted recommendation can lead to several problems, such as being too vague, difficult to complete, or not addressing the causes or contributors identified in the investigation. It might also fail to gain buy-in from the organisation or other key stakeholders.

SMART Actions

For some internal work health and safety investigators, there will be a requirement to develop corrective actions instead of, or alongside, recommendations. If that is the case, those recommendations should be SMART. SMART is an acronym for Specific, Measurable, Achievable, Realistic, and Time-bound. SMART criteria ensure actions are clear and actionable:

Specific: The action should be clear and unambiguous. It should define exactly what needs to be done, where, and how.

Measurable: There should be clear criteria for determining when the action has been completed.

Achievable: The action should be assignable to an individual who has the authority and resources to complete it.

Realistic: The action should be feasible within the given timeframe.

Time-bound: The action should have a clear deadline.

Example of a SMART action

Susan, the Operations Manager, must oversee the replacement of non-slip mats in all six production areas, ensuring completion by close of business on Friday, 19 July 2024.

Reviewing this action:

Is it Specific? Yes – it clearly defines what needs to be done.

Is it Measurable? Yes – we will know if the non-slip mats have been replaced.

Is it Achievable? Yes – assuming Susan is capable, this action is within her ability.

Is it Realistic? Yes – replacing mat flooring should be realistic, and even routine.

Is it Time-bound? Yes – it has a deadline by close of business on Friday, 19 July 2024.

Non-SMART Actions

All personnel to wear hard hats at all times.

Is it Specific? No – it does not specify who "all personnel" are or what "at all times" means.

Is it Measurable? No – there is no point in the future when it can be considered complete.

Is it Achievable? No – it is not assigned to a specific person.

Is it Realistic? No – it's unrealistic to expect that personnel will always wear hard hats, even in situations where it might be necessary.

Is it Time-bound? No – there is no deadline.

Turning Non-SMART Actions into SMART Actions

Here are examples of how non-SMART actions can be revised:

Non-SMART: "All personnel to wear hard hats at all times."

SMART: "The Manager must conduct a safety briefing for operational staff on the mandatory use of hard hats while on the factory floor. The briefing must be completed by close of business on Friday, 19 July 2024."

Non-SMART: "Improve communication."

SMART: "The project manager must develop a weekly schedule of meetings with the client for the duration of the project. The weekly meeting agenda must specify feedback to and from the client regarding safety practices on site. The schedule should be sent to the client for confirmation by close of business each Thursday."

Despite their effectiveness, SMART actions have limitations. They may not incorporate the hierarchy of controls, consider change management steps, or account for the risks associated with the action. Furthermore, SMART actions may lack context, complicating future reviews.

Further Considerations for Recommendations

To avoid ineffective recommendations, consider the following:

- Avoid repeat or 'Re-' actions: Avoid repeating recommendations that have already been tried, such as re-communicating, re-training, or reinforcing existing policies.

- Focus on engineering change: Consider engineering a change to the context, conditions, or environment to address the finding.

- Consider barriers to the recommendations: Ask what factors could hinder the prevention of similar incidents in the future?

- Disclaimer: An external workplace incident investigator will need to ensure their recommendations are treated as such by the organisation that has engaged them. The organisation retains responsibility for adopting and implementing recommendations. External workplace incident investigators should clarify this through a formal disclaimer.

For internal investigations, the organisation should have a system for recording and tracking the implementation of recommendations and actions to ensure they are addressed and reviewed. External workplace incident investigators may not be responsible for this, but it's crucial for the organisation to have a robust system in place.

28 | Investigation Bias — Revisited

At this stage, it is essential for the workplace incident investigator to critically reflect on their thoughts and how these might have influenced the investigation. Revisiting the list of biases outlined in the appendix and re-examining the initial statement from the chapter on Biases can provide valuable insights. This reflective practice is valuable across all investigative approaches—whether traditional, root cause-based, or learning-oriented—as it supports deeper insight into context, reasoning, and sense-making. The workplace incident should document reflections guided by the following questions.

- What have you learned that you did not know before the investigation?

Reflect on whether the investigation confirmed pre-existing beliefs or uncovered new information. This assesses whether the process was exploratory or confirmatory.

- Why did it make sense for the person or persons to do what they did?

Consider the decisions and actions of those involved from an empathetic perspective. This aligns with the principle of local rationality, which asks: given the information, pressures, and goals at the time, how did the actions make sense to the person? Could the workplace incident investigator advocate for or justify their actions? This encourages empathy and a deeper understanding of the context and motivations behind their actions.

- What surprised you during the investigation?

Identifying unexpected findings reveals where the investigator's assumptions were challenged. This can be a key indicator of the investigation's thoroughness.

- What would make avoiding this incident in the future extremely difficult?

This question helps identify systemic or deeply ingrained issues that may not be easily resolved. Recognising these challenges is key to developing effective recommendations.

- How have you made sense of conflicting information?

Investigations often involve conflicting accounts, particularly in witness statements. The workplace incident investigator should reflect on how they reconciled these differences and what methods they used to determine the most meaningful version of events.

Carefully considering these questions helps the workplace incident investigator identify biases that may have influenced their conclusions. This reflection also assists the workplace incident investigator to remain open to new perspectives, avoiding the constraints of initial assumptions.

Language and conscious reflection on thoughts and assumptions are critical to a successful investigation. They influence how the investigation is perceived, how participants engage with it, and ultimately, how effective the resulting recommendations will be. For learning-oriented investigations in particular, this conscious reflection forms the bedrock of creating shared understanding and trust—essential for sustaining engagement and meaningful change.

29 | Investigation Reporting

The purpose of a workplace incident investigation should guide the content, tone, and structure of the investigation report. Understanding the purpose will help identify the intended audience, which could range from lawyers and board members to workers, the health and safety team, clients, or contractors. Tailoring the report to meet each audience's specific needs is crucial.

It is also important to understand that an investigation report is merely one version of what happened. It represents an interpretation of events based on the available evidence and may not encompass the entirety of objective reality. For this reason, the language used in the report should be chosen carefully. the wording of the report should reflect its limitations and subjectivity. Definitive statements should be minimised to reflect the investigation's inherent limitations. This applies equally to system-based investigations and learning-focused methods. In all approaches, the final output is shaped by the evidence gathered, the method applied, and the interpretive lens of those involved.

Key Components of the Investigation Report

While the following structure applies primarily to formal investigative reporting, alternative approaches may produce reports with different formats—such as learning summaries or shared reflection outputs—that still serve the purpose of capturing insights and supporting improvement. An effective investigation report should include the following components to ensure clarity and actionability.

- Incident ID Number: A unique identifier for the incident to distinguish it from others, crucial for tracking and for referencing the incident.

- Incident Date: The exact date of the incident, providing context and timing for the events described.

- Incident Description: A detailed account of the incident, including the location and consequences. This should be written in plain language, providing a clear picture of what happened, where it occurred, and its immediate impact. Where multiple incidents are identified, include multiple descriptions.

- Immediate Action Taken: A summary of the immediate responses or interventions following the incident, which could include emergency measures, initial communications, or temporary controls put in place.

- Names of Persons Involved: Include full names, titles, and affiliations of all individuals involved in the incident, including witnesses and any involved persons. This ensures clarity about who was present and their roles.

- Purpose of the Investigation: Clearly state the investigation's purpose. For example, if the investigation is conducted "to obtain legal advice," this should be explicitly noted, as it influences the scope and confidentiality of the report.

- Lead Workplace Incident Investigator and Bio: Include the name and a brief biography of the lead workplace incident investigator, establishing credibility and expertise in conducting the investigation.

- Investigation Brief: A summary of the investigation's scope, objectives, and any specific instructions provided by the person or organisation that commissioned the investigation.

- Initial Bias Statement: A declaration of the workplace incident investigator's thoughts and potential influences at the start of the investigation. This transparency helps to contextualise the findings and recommendations.

- Limitations of the Investigation: Detail any constraints that may have influenced the investigation, including:

  - Witnesses who were unable to be interviewed, and the reasons for that.
  - Evidence that was inaccessible, damaged, tampered with, or otherwise unusable.
  - The impact of time delays on the availability or reliability of evidence.
  - Budget constraints, such as for engaging specialists for monitoring.
  - Resourcing constraints, such as a lack of access to expert witnesses (as defined in this book).

- **Timeline of Events**: A chronological account of the events leading up to and following the incident. It is important to identify and redact any private or confidential information where necessary to protect sensitive data.

- **Investigation Analysis Team**: List the full names, titles, and affiliations of the individuals involved in the analysis phase of the investigation. This ensures accountability and identifies contributors to the findings.

- **Causation Analysis Reasoning and Findings: Include** in this section a determination of whether the incident was a one-off departure from standard practice or indicative of a systemic failure. Consistent with safety literature (e.g., Kletz), causal terminology should be used cautiously. It is more helpful to frame findings in terms of 'factors contributing to the incident'.

- **Recommendations**: Recommendations should link directly to the causation analysis reasoning and findings. Where appropriate, recommendations should align with broader organisational learning approaches, including feedback loops and opportunities for co-designed improvements with frontline teams. This section should offer well-thought-out recommendations that include:

- ○ Reference to the hierarchy of controls to ensure that recommendations follow best practice in risk management.

- ○ Change management steps to ensure that recommended actions are sustainable and effectively implemented.

- ○ Any additional recommendations, provided they are within the scope defined by the person or organisation that commissioned the report.

- **Signature of Lead Workplace Incident Investigator**: The report should be signed by the lead workplace incident investigator.

- **Appendices**: Include supporting documents such as:

- ○ Witness interview statements (anonymised where appropriate to maintain compliance with privacy laws.).

- ○ The workplace incident investigator's interview statements following witness interviews.

Note: Any private or confidential information should be carefully reviewed. If necessary, the appendices should list the document's title but indicate that it has not been included for privacy or confidentiality reasons.

The report must comply with legal and organisational document retention requirements. This is crucial for future reference, legal proceedings, or audits.

Following this structured approach ensures the report is comprehensive, clear, and tailored to its intended audience and purpose.

Further Topics:
Due Diligence Through Workplace Inquiries

"The Board requests an inquiry into..."[29]

The inclusion of this phrase in Board minutes signals the Board's commitment to rigorous oversight and accountability in health and safety governance. For the Board and organisational officers, commissioning workplace incident investigations is not only an obligation but also a strategic tool to demonstrate due diligence under health and safety laws. This chapter explores how workplace incident investigations serve as robust inquiry mechanisms for Boards to meet their due diligence obligations using the tools outlined in this book selectively. These inquiry mechanisms may take various forms—including traditional investigations, independent reviews, or learning review-style debriefs—and the core investigative principles outlined in this book apply to each, with adjustments as needed.

Boards should approach workplace investigations as layered inquiries—peeling back surface issues to explore deeper organisational dynamics. This reflects Kletz's[30] 'onion' model of learning from accidents, which emphasises the need to look beyond the immediate to the systemic.

---

[29] Greg Smith, NZISM Roadshow, 2024.

[30] Kletz, T (2001) *Learning from Accidents.*

In many jurisdictions, Boards and organisation officers are bound by a positive duty under health and safety laws to ensure that their organisations implement effective safety systems. This duty typically requires Boards and organisation officers to:

- Understand their organisation's crucial systems.

- Verify the effectiveness of those crucial systems.

- Ensure that the ongoing information available to them informs them of the effectiveness of those crucial systems.

Failure to uphold these standards can result in severe consequences, including serious incidents, legal action, and reputational damage. Insufficient Board oversight based on misplaced trust in operational management, superficial reliance on process, and a lack of informed inquiry, can lead to catastrophic failure.

Workplace investigations commissioned by Boards are proactive inquiry measures that go beyond routine audits and dashboard reports. Unlike compliance checks focused solely on metrics, well-structured inquiries assess the effectiveness of crucial systems regardless of whether a linear root-cause model is used or whether a more emergent, systems-based or adaptive inquiry method is adopted. These inquiries assess whether systems are not only present but also functional and resilient, serving as essential tools for demonstrating due diligence.

Key Components of Effective Due Diligence Inquiries

1. Alignment on crucial systems

- The Board and the organisation's officers should share a clear understanding of what the organisation's crucial systems are.

- Defining Purpose: Boards must clearly define the purpose of the inquiry—whether to investigate a specific incident, assess risk controls, or evaluate operational safety.

- Scope of Inquiry: Clearly specify which safety processes or departments will be examined, leveraging previous incidents or high-risk areas as focus points.

2. Independent Verification

- Boards should ensure that due diligence inquiries incorporate independent oversight, where appropriate, such as third-party audits or expert assessments.

3. Comprehensive Evidence Collection

- Collect a range of evidence types, including documented protocols, witness statements, and data from safety system tests. This multi-source approach provides a clearer picture of the organisation's practices.

- Challenge and verify the documentary evidence by questioning those involved in its development. Each document should have an 'oral sponsor' who can verify its contents and address any assumptions on which it is based.

4. Organisational Memory and Dissemination

- Boards and officers should ensure that inquiry findings are widely shared, lessons institutionalised, and the corporate memory actively maintained. Without this, even well-run inquiries risk fading into irrelevance over time.

For an inquiry to effectively demonstrate due diligence, the Board must:

- Consider and, where appropriate, act on inquiry findings and recommendations.

- Verify that meaningful change has resulted from the implemented recommendations.

Commissioning and participating in workplace incident inquiries is one of the most effective ways for a Board or organisational officer to demonstrate due diligence. The phrase 'The Board requests an inquiry into...' should be regularly included in Board minutes, and acted upon. These inquiries should utilise the investigation tools and evidence assessment techniques outlined in this book to evaluate the efficacy of crucial systems, align with best practices, and incorporate independent perspectives where appropriate.

Further Topics: AI in Workplace Incident Investigations

"AI Generated; Human Verified"[31]

Artificial Intelligence (AI) has swept across industries, transforming processes and redefining the nature of work. Its application in workplace incident investigations—whether traditional, systems-based, or learning-focused— is no exception. While AI has the potential to make investigations faster, more comprehensive, and more efficient, it also brings with it a host of implications—some promising and others concerning. This chapter looks at the benefits, biases, and risks that AI introduces into the realm of workplace incident investigations, drawing on recent discussions about AI's capabilities and ethical considerations.

AI can process vast amounts of data with speed and accuracy unattainable by human investigators. Whether it is analysing video footage, identifying patterns in safety records, or assessing voice recordings for stress indicators during witness interviews, AI's ability to sift through complex datasets is unparalleled This capability can be invaluable to workplace incident investigators tasked with quickly and thoroughly determining the causes and contributing factors of incidents.

---

[31] Anonymous.

For instance, AI-powered video analytics can monitor and analyse hours of workplace footage, flagging unsafe behaviours, potential hazards, and near-misses that may have been overlooked by human eyes. This real-time analysis can contribute to proactive safety measures, preventing incidents before they occur. AI-assisted report generation, drawing on structured data from various sources, can make initial findings clearer and more actionable, freeing investigators from the time-consuming task of manual data compilation.

However, the introduction of AI into workplace investigations is not without its challenges. One of the most critical issues is bias. AI machines learn from the data they are fed and reflect the biases inherent in that data. If an AI system is trained on biased data or designed with certain assumptions, it may inadvertently reinforce discriminatory practices or skew investigation results.

Biases embedded in AI systems can originate from historical data reflecting existing inequities or from oversights in system training. Workplace incident investigators must understand that while AI can highlight trends and offer insights, it can also project biased interpretations of events if not carefully monitored and calibrated.

The use of AI in workplace incident investigations also brings up significant ethical concerns related to data privacy and surveillance. Data gathered by AI systems must be stored and managed with the utmost care to comply with privacy regulations. The potential for misuse or unauthorised access to sensitive data poses a risk that could lead to serious breaches of trust and legal challenges. AI may access private or confidential data and share it without indicating its sensitive nature.

One of the most profound implications of using AI in workplace incident investigations is the challenge of distinguishing between truth and manipulated information. AI presents data and conclusions with persuasive confidence, which can be both beneficial and misleading. When AI suggests findings, there is a risk that investigators, especially those with limited understanding of the AI's workings, may accept these conclusions without proper scrutiny. This is especially true in approaches like learning reviews or narrative inquiries, where meaning is constructed through dialogue, context, and human interpretation, not algorithmic outputs.

The phenomenon of AI generating confident but incorrect answers is well-documented and stems from how AI models interpret and present data. Therefore, workplace incident investigators must strike a balance between leveraging AI's analytical power and applying human oversight to ensure that findings are grounded and not simply data-driven assumptions.

AI Generated; Human Verified

Harnessing AI's benefits while mitigating risks requires ethical training, transparent practices, and continuous human oversight. Workplace incident investigators must understand not only the capabilities but also the limitations of AI tools. This training should focus on recognising when to question AI outputs and apply human judgement to refine or validate findings.

Organisations should commit to implementing AI systems within an ethical framework that prioritises fairness and accountability. This commitment includes selecting transparent AI systems whose decision-making logic can be audited and explained. This includes choosing transparent AI models where the logic behind decisions can be audited and explained. Open-source tools and collaborative.

Workplace incident investigators should use AI, but only after they have performed their own careful analysis. AI's output can be used to cross-reference findings or prompt their reassessment by the workplace incident investigator. The workplace incident investigator's own analysis should come first. The AI analysis should follow. The AI's analysis should only be used as a verification tool. It should not be used as a substitute.

AI presents new opportunities in workplace investigations, offering enhanced efficiency and deeper data analysis. Yet, it also comes with the critical responsibility of ensuring that these tools are used ethically and without bias. Workplace incident investigators must use AI cautiously, not as mere operators but as thoughtful partners aware of its broader implications.

The true challenge lies in blending human empathy, ethical awareness, and machine intelligence. Workplace incident investigators, as ethical stewards of AI, will shape whether this technology promotes safety or exacerbates ethical and privacy issues.

This chapter has been informed in part by publicly available materials including *"Mo Gawdat on AI: The Future of AI and How It Will Shape Our World"* and Henrik Kniberg *"Generative AI in a Nutshell - how to survive and thrive in the age of AI"*, which offer clear and accessible explanations of the promises and risks of generative AI.

Links:

- Mo Gawdat on AI: The Future of AI and How It Will Shape Our World: https://www.youtube.com/watch?v=HhcNrnNJY54

- Generative AI in a Nutshell - how to survive and thrive in the age of AI: https://www.youtube.com/watch?v=2IK3DFHRFfw

Bibliography and Further Reading

I recommend the following resources for further information on investigation tools, techniques, methodologies and models.

Australian Institute of Health and Safety (AIHS) Body of Knowledge Chapters:

Dell, G., Toft, Y., Cikara, I., Skegg, D., & Dell, S. (2024). Investigations. In Australian Institute of Health & Safety, The core body of knowledge for generalist OHS professionals (3rd ed.). https://www.ohsbok.org.au/bok-chapters/.

Dell, G., Toft, Y., Cikara, I., Skegg, D., & Dell, S. (2024). Guide to effective investigations. In Australian Institute of Health & Safety, The core body of knowledge for generalist OHS professionals. (3rd ed.). https://www.ohsbok.org.au/bok-chapters/.

Pryor, P., Capra, M. (2012). Foundation Science. In HaSPA (Health and Safety Professionals Alliance), The Core Body of Knowledge for Generalist OHS Professionals. Tullamarine, VIC. Safety Institute of Australia.

Books and articles from leading safety thinkers:

Anand, Nippin (2024) *Are we Learning from Accidents?: A quandary, a question and a way forward*. Novellus.

Long, Robert (2016) *Conversations, The Law, Social Psychology and Risk*. Scotoma Press.

Smith, Greg (2018) *Papersafe*. Wayland Legal Pty Ltd.

Smith, Greg (2024) *Proving Safety*. Wayland Legal Pty Ltd.

Other readings and resources consulted for this book:

Douglas W. Hubbard (2020). *The Failure of Risk Management: Why it's broken and how to fix it*, 2nd ed. John Wiley & Sons, Inc.

Ferry, TS *Modern Accident Investigation and Analysis: Second Edition* (1988) John Wiley and Sons, Inc.

Hollnagel, E., & Macleod, F. (2019) The imperfections of accident analysis. in *Loss Prevention Bulletin*, 270(3), 2-6.

Howe, ML, & Knott, LM (2015). The fallibility of memory in judicial processes: lessons from the past and their modern consequences. *Memory (Hove, England)*, 23(5), 633–656. https://doi.org/10.1080/09658211.2015.1010709.

Hughes, Chase (2017) *The Ellipses Manual: Analysis and Engineering of Human Behaviour*. Evergreen Press, Virginia.

Kenny, K. E. (2015). Blaming Deadmen: Causes, Culprits, and Chaos in Accounting for Technological Accidents. *Science, Technology, & Human Values*, *40*(4), 539–563. https://doi.org/10.1177/0162243914559288.

Kletz, Trevor (2001) *Learning from Accidents*. 3rd Edition. Routledge.

MacLean, C. L., & Miller, G. S. (2024). Trust but verify: The biasing effects of witness opinions and background knowledge in workplace investigations. *Journal of Safety Research*, Volume 89.

Manuele, Fred A. (2008) Serious Injuries & Fatalities A Call for a New Focus on Their Prevention. *Prof. Safety* 53.

Mehrabian, A (1971) *Silent Messages*. University of California.

Rae, A.J., McDermid, J.A., Alexander, R.D., Nicholson, M. (2014) Probative blindness: how safety activity can fail to update beliefs about safety, in: *9th IET International Conference on System Safety and Cyber Security* (2014).

de Boer, Robert. (2021). *Safety Leadership: A Different, Doable and Directed Approach to Operational Improvements.* 10.1201/9781003143338.

Ross, David (2007) *Advocacy* Cambridge, Cambridge University Press.

Schollum, Mary (2005) *Investigative Interviewing: The Literature.* Wellington, New Zealand Police.

Thorley, C., & Rushton-Woods, J. (2013). Blame conformity: Leading eyewitness statements can influence attributions of blame for an accident. *Applied cognitive psychology*, 27(3), 291-296.

Vesel, C. (2020). Agentive language in accident investigation: Why language matters in learning from events. *ACS Chemical Health & Safety*, 27(1), 34-39.

Woods, D and Cook, R (1999) *Perspectives on Human Error: Hindsight Bias and Local Rationality*. https://www.researchgate.net/profile/David-Woods-19/publication/251196331_Perspectives_on_Human_Error_Hindsight_Biases_and_Local_Rationality/links/567815d108aebcdda0ebbbc3/Perspectives-on-Human-Error-Hindsight-Biases-and-Local-Rationality.pdf

WorkSafe BC (2016) *Reference Guide for Employer Incident Investigations*. https://www.worksafebc.com/en/resources/health-safety/books-guides/investigations-accidents-incidents-reference-guide-and-workbook?lang=en.

Appendix 1
Investigation Bias List

Cognitive biases can profoundly impact the accuracy and objectivity of workplace health and safety incident investigations. These biases, which are mental shortcuts or tendencies that influence decision-making, can lead to errors in decision-making that may impact decisions significantly, potentially raising legal or compliance issues if not identified and mitigated. As such, it is crucial for workplace incident investigators to be aware of these biases and actively work to mitigate their effects.

Cognitive biases often manifest during investigations, frequently without the workplace incident investigator's awareness.

Acknowledging and Mitigating Biases

Acknowledging the existence and potential impact of cognitive biases is the first step in addressing them during investigations. It is important to recognise that everyone, regardless of expertise or experience, has biases. Workplace incident investigators should reflect on their own, known biases and consider how these might influence their interpretation of evidence and decision-making.

Bias Blind Spots

- Ethical Issues: This is the belief that bias affects only corrupt or unscrupulous individuals, framing it as a moral issue linked to personal integrity.

- Bad Apples: The assumption that bias is a result of incompetence and only affects those who do not know how to do their job properly.

- Expert Immunity: The notion that experts are impartial and immune to bias because of their competence and integrity.

- Technological Protections: The belief that technology, automation, or artificial intelligence can eliminate human biases entirely.

- Blind Spot Bias: The conviction that other experts are susceptible to bias, but not oneself— with the belief that 'I am objective, while others may be biased.'

- Illusion of Control: The assumption that awareness of bias allows one to control and counteract its effects through sheer willpower.

Workplace incident investigators should be cautious when analysing specific investigation data, such as photographs, documents, or other evidence. They should ensure that the investigation moves from evidence to theory, not the other way around, to avoid circular reasoning.

Cognitive biases are a significant challenge in workplace incident investigations, but by acknowledging their presence and mitigating their impact, workplace incident investigators can conduct more meaningful investigations.

Below is a list of known biases, a description of what they are, and an example of how that bias might affect a workplace incident investigator.

Name	Description	Example
Actor-observer bias	The tendency for explanations of other individuals' behaviours to overemphasise the influence of their personality and underemphasise the influence of their situation. It can extend to explanations of one's own behaviours to do the opposite (that is, to overemphasise the influence of our situation and underemphasise the influence of our own personality.	A workplace incident investigator might attribute the limitations of obtaining evidence from a witness to the witness's behaviour, instead of their own ability to obtain evidence from a witness during an interview.
Agent detection	The inclination to presume purposeful intent.	A workplace incident investigator might erroneously attribute a safety incident to reckless acts by a worker, interpreting ambiguous evidence like misplaced tools as intentional rather than accidental.
Ambiguity effect	The tendency to avoid options for which the probability of a favourable outcome is unknown.	A workplace incident investigator might avoid investigating an aspect of the incident that seems unclear or lacks concrete data, such as the influence of deadlines on workers taking shortcuts.
Anchoring or focalism	Anchoring bias is the tendency to rely too heavily on the first piece of information encountered when making decisions, even if that information is irrelevant or inaccurate.	A workplace incident investigator might fixate on the initial report that the involved person was behaving erratically, allowing this piece of information to disproportionately influence their subsequent analysis. This bias can skew the investigation towards scrutinising the IP's past rather than objectively evaluating all evidence.
Attentional bias	The tendency of perception to be affected by recurring thoughts.	A workplace incident investigator might focus disproportionately on a recent high-profile incident involving heavy machinery, overlooking subtler, systemic safety issues in other areas.

Name	Description	Example
Attribute substitution	Occurs when a judgement must be made (of a target attribute) that is computationally complex, and instead a more easily calculated heuristic attribute is substituted.	A workplace incident investigator might assume that a worker's lack of attention caused an incident, rather than considering how workplace conditions or procedures may have contributed to the incident.
Authority bias	The tendency to attribute greater accuracy to the opinion of an authority figure (unrelated to its content) and be more influenced by that opinion.	A workplace incident investigator might give undue weight to the opinions of expert witnesses or senior management witnesses, even when evidence suggests alternative conclusions.
Automation bias	The tendency to depend excessively on automated systems which can lead to erroneous automated information overriding correct decisions.	A workplace incident investigator may overly trust data from environmental monitoring and disregard conflicting evidence from employee reports.
Availability cascade	A self-reinforcing process in which a collective belief gains more and more plausibility through its increasing repetition in public discourse (or "repeat something long enough and it will become true").	If the workplace has a history of time pressure on production, the workplace incident investigator might come to believe it as most significant threat, regardless of actual risk data.
Availability heuristic	Availability bias is the tendency to rely on readily available information when making decisions, rather than considering all available evidence.	If a workplace incident investigator has personally witnessed multiple cases of worker error leading to incidents, they may instinctively blame human mistakes in future investigations, even when evidence suggests that systemic failures (e.g., poor equipment maintenance or unclear procedures) are more causative.
Backfire effect	The reaction to disconfirming evidence by strengthening one's previous beliefs.	A workplace incident investigator might strongly believe that a specific piece of equipment is inherently safe and becomes more convinced of its safety despite new evidence showing its flaws.

Name	Description	Example
Bandwagon effect	The tendency to do (or believe) things because many other people do (or believe) the same. Related to groupthink and herd behaviour.	An Investigation Analysis Team may collectively agree that the incident was caused by a lack of worker competency because that conclusion aligns with the known views of the organisation's senior management.
Base rate fallacy or Base rate neglect	The tendency to ignore general information and focus on information only pertaining to the specific case, even when the general information is more important.	A workplace incident investigator might overlook statistical data showing that most similar workplace incidents are due to environmental factors, focusing instead on rare equipment malfunctions.
Belief bias	An effect where someone's evaluation of the logical strength of an argument is biased by the believability of the conclusion.	A workplace incident investigator who believes that seasoned employees are less likely to make mistakes might dismiss evidence of human error from a senior worker.
Berkson's paradox	The tendency to misinterpret statistical experiments involving conditional probabilities.	If a workplace incident investigator notices that injuries occur more frequently among new employees than experienced workers, they may conclude that experience alone prevents injuries. However, this could be because employees who have suffered injuries early in their careers are more likely to leave the industry, leaving a survivor bias where only the safest workers remain.
Choice-supportive bias	The tendency to remember one's choices as better than they were.	The workplace incident investigator may rely on the perceived success of past recommendations, overlooking whether the context remains applicable.

Name	Description	Example
Clustering illusion	The tendency to overestimate the importance of small runs, streaks, or clusters in large samples of random data (that is, seeing phantom patterns).	If a company experiences multiple hand injuries in a short period, a workplace incident investigator may assume that there is a major problem with hand safety. However, broader data may reveal that other injury types (e.g., back strains, falls) are just as common but are being overlooked due to a short-term spike in hand injuries.
Compassion fade	The predisposition to behave more compassionately towards a small number of identifiable victims than too many anonymous ones.	A workplace incident investigator might push for immediate safety improvements after hearing an emotional firsthand account from an injured worker but fail to address broader, systemic risks affecting many other employees in less visible ways.
Confirmation bias	The tendency to search for, interpret, focus on and remember information in a way that confirms one's preconceptions. Also referred to as 'what you look for is what you find'.	A workplace incident investigator who suspects poor training as the cause of an incident might only seek evidence supporting this view, ignoring contrary information.
Congruence bias	The tendency to test hypotheses exclusively through direct testing, instead of testing possible alternative hypotheses.	If a workplace incident investigator believes that incidents happen because workers fail to follow procedures, they may only look for evidence of procedural non-compliance. They may overlook alternative explanations, such as poorly designed workflows, production pressures, or unclear instructions.
Conservatism (belief revision)	The tendency to revise one's belief insufficiently when presented with new evidence.	A workplace incident investigator might cling to initial conclusions despite new, conflicting evidence that suggests a different cause for an incident.

Name	Description	Example
Continued influence effect	The tendency to believe previously learned misinformation even after it has been corrected.	Even after being presented with evidence that an incident was caused by systemic failures (e.g., poor equipment maintenance or unclear procedures), a workplace incident investigator might still attribute the cause to worker error because they were initially told that the worker made a mistake.
Contrast effect	The enhancement or reduction of a certain stimulus' perception when compared with a recently observed, contrasting object.	A workplace incident investigator might overemphasise the role of older machinery in an incident, especially when compared to newly upgraded equipment with no issues, leading them to attribute the incident primarily to the equipment's age, potentially overlooking other contributing factors like maintenance practices or operator training.
Courtesy bias	The tendency to give an opinion that is more socially correct than one's true opinion, to avoid offending anyone.	A workplace incident investigator might downplay their concerns about safety practices during discussions with management to avoid conflict or offense.
Curse of knowledge	When better-informed people find it extremely difficult to think about problems from the perspective of lesser-informed people.	A workplace incident investigator with extensive equipment experience might assume that the operator in question understands that equipment to the same technical level, leading to inaccurate weighting of that witness's evidence.
Declinism	The predisposition to view the past favourably (rosy retrospection) and future negatively.	A workplace incident investigator might believe that safety culture in the organisation has worsened over the years, focusing on recent incidents and disregarding long term, gradual improvements.

Name	Description	Example
Decoy effect	Preferences for either option A or B change in favour of option B when option C is presented, which is completely dominated by option B (inferior in all respects) and partially dominated by option A.	A workplace incident investigator might be aware of two courses of action an involved person could have taken. But an expert witness makes the workplace incident investigator aware of a third option. This could cause the workplace incident investigator to form an inaccurate counter-factual 'necessary condition test' in their causation analysis.
Default effect	When given a choice between several options, the tendency to favour the default one.	A workplace incident investigator might rely on pre-prepared witness interview outcomes, rather than revising this as the investigation continues.
Defensive attribution hypothesis	Attributing more blame to a harm-doer as the outcome becomes more severe or as personal or situational similarity to the victim increases.	A workplace incident investigator might attribute the cause of a forklift related injury to the forklift operator, especially if the investigator also operated forklifts. By attributing the incident solely to the operator's error, the investigator distances themselves from the idea that they could also make the same mistake.
Distinction bias	The tendency to view two options as more dissimilar when evaluating them simultaneously than when evaluating them separately.	When comparing two safety incidents to determine a possible systemic issue, a workplace incident investigator might focus on minor differences and overlook their overall similarity and common causes.
Dunning–Kruger effect	The tendency for unskilled individuals to overestimate their own ability and the tendency for experts to underestimate their own ability.	An inexperienced workplace incident investigator might overestimate their ability to evaluate and weight witnesses' evidence, missing critical details and misinterpreting evidence.

Name	Description	Example
Empathy gap	The tendency to underestimate the influence or strength of feelings, in either oneself or others.	A workplace incident investigator might struggle to understand the stress and fear experienced by workers during an incident, leading to an incomplete assessment of human factors.
Exaggerated expectation	The tendency to expect or predict more extreme outcomes than those outcomes that actually happen.	A workplace incident investigator might have unrealistic expectations about the impact of a new safety protocol, leading to disappointment and potential abandonment when results are less than expected.
Experimenter's or expectation bias	The tendency for experimenters to believe, certify, and publish data that agree with their expectations for the outcome of an experiment, and to disbelieve, discard, or downgrade the corresponding weightings for data that appear to conflict with those expectations.	A workplace incident investigator might unintentionally influence the outcome of an investigation to align with their expectations, such as a finding that a cause is lack of resourcing for a project and focusing on finding evidence for that cause.
Extrinsic incentives bias	When people view others as having (situational) extrinsic motivations and (dispositional) intrinsic motivations for oneself	A workplace incident investigator might assume that workers' non-compliance with safe operating procedures is primarily driven by external rewards or penalties, overlooking motivations like peer influence.
False consensus effect	The tendency for people to overestimate the degree to which others agree with them.	A workplace incident investigator might overestimate the extent to which others shared their views on safety culture, assuming their recommendations are universally accepted.
False uniqueness bias	The tendency of people to see their projects and themselves as more singular than they actually are.	A workplace incident investigator might believe their understanding of an expert witness's perspective is unique and superior, underestimating the value of other witnesses.

Name	Description	Example
Focusing effect	The tendency to place too much importance on one aspect of an event.	A workplace incident investigator might focus excessively on a single factor, like machine maintenance, while neglecting other important aspects such as worker competence.
Framing effect	Drawing different conclusions from the same information, depending on how that information is presented.	The way a workplace incident investigator might use subjective language to describe an incident, which can influence how others perceive its severity and the urgency of response.
Frequency illusion or Baader–Meinhof phenomenon	The frequency illusion is that once something has been noticed then every instance of that thing is noticed, leading to the belief it has a high frequency of occurrence (a form of selection bias).	After learning about a specific type of safety hazard, and workplace incident investigator might start noticing it more frequently, believing it's more common than it is.
Functional fixedness	Limits a person to using an object only in the way it is traditionally used.	A workplace incident investigator might rely only on a single, popular investigation methodology and not consider alternative methods.
Gambler's fallacy	The tendency to think that future probabilities are altered by past events, when in reality they are unchanged. The fallacy arises from an erroneous conceptualisation of the law of large numbers.	During an investigation of a recent workplace incident, a safety investigator might believe that the incident occurred because the department had gone an unusually long time without any incidents, thinking they were "due" for one.
Group attribution error	The biased belief that the characteristics of an individual group member are reflective of the group as a whole or the tendency to assume that group decision outcomes reflect the preferences of group members, even when information is available that clearly suggests otherwise.	A workplace incident investigator might generalise the behaviour or characteristics of one group of workers based on the actions of a few individuals, such as assuming a cohort of newly hired workers all share the same characteristics.

Name	Description	Example
Groupthink	The psychological phenomenon that occurs within a group of people in which the desire for harmony or conformity in the group results in an irrational or dysfunctional decision-making outcome.	Within an Investigation Analysis Team, the workplace incident investigator might go along with the majority opinion even if they have doubts, to avoid conflict and maintain harmony.
Halo effect	The tendency for a person's positive or negative traits to "spill over" from one personality area to another in others' perceptions of them.	A workplace incident investigator might let positive impressions of a manager influence their judgement of causation, assuming that a well-liked individual is also more safety conscious.
Hindsight bias	Sometimes called the "I-knew-it-all-along" effect, the tendency to see past events as being predictable at the time those events happened.	A workplace incident investigator might assume that the cause of an incident was obvious after the fact, when there were many possible causes that, at the time, were not apparent.
Hostile attribution bias	The "hostile attribution bias" is the tendency to interpret others' behaviours as having hostile intent, even when the behaviour is ambiguous or benign.	A workplace incident investigator might interpret a worker's mistake as a deliberate act of negligence or defiance rather than an error or honest mistake.
Illicit transference	Occurs when a term in the distributive (referring to every member of a class) and collective (referring to the class itself as a whole) sense are treated as equivalent. The two variants of this fallacy are the fallacy of composition and the fallacy of division.	A workplace incident investigator might conclude that because individual workers follow safety protocols, the workplace as a whole is safe. However, systemic issues like poor safety culture, ineffective supervision, or lack of proper equipment maintenance may still create significant risks.

Name	Description	Example
Illusion of control	The tendency to overestimate one's degree of influence over other external events.	A workplace incident investigator might believe that an incident occurred because the workers did not follow safety protocols closely enough, thinking that their strict enforcement of rules would have completely prevented the incident.
Illusion of transparency	People overestimate others' ability to know themselves, and they also overestimate their ability to know others.	The workplace incident investigator might assume that workers involved in an incident will openly disclose all key details. However, workers might withhold information due to fear of blame, uncertainty about what is relevant, or assumptions that the investigator already knows the details.
Illusion of validity	Believing that one's judgements are accurate, especially when available information is consistent or inter-correlated.	A workplace incident investigator might place undue confidence in their judgement about the cause of an incident, even when evidence is consistent but limited or ambiguous.
Illusory correlation	Inaccurately perceiving a relationship between two unrelated events.	A workplace incident investigator might notice that incidents occurred mostly on days when temporary workers were present and incorrectly conclude that the temporary staff are causing the incidents. However, this perceived relationship between temporary workers and incidents could be coincidental, with the real cause stemming from equipment problems.
Illusory truth effect	A tendency to believe that a statement is true if it is easier to process, or if it has been stated multiple times, regardless of its actual veracity.	If a workplace incident investigator repeatedly hears from colleagues that a certain manager is focussed heavily on production deadlines, they might start believing it despite a lack of evidence.

Name	Description	Example
Information bias	The tendency to seek information even when it cannot affect action.	A workplace incident investigator might collect excessive and unnecessary data, believing that more information will always lead to better conclusions. This bias can lead to 'analysis paralysis' and cause undue delay in finalising the investigation.
In-group bias	The tendency for people to give preferential treatment to others they perceive to be members of their own groups.	A workplace incident investigator might give more weight to the evidence of a witness that is doing a task the workplace incident investigator once did in the past.
Intentionality bias	Tendency to judge human action as intentional rather than accidental.	A workplace incident investigator might assume that safety violations are intentional acts of defiance rather than mistakes or misunderstandings.
Irrational escalation or Escalation of commitment (the sunk cost fallacy)	The phenomenon where people justify increased investment in a decision, based on the cumulative prior investment, despite new evidence suggesting that the decision was probably wrong.	A workplace incident investigator might continue to invest time and resources into pursuing a line of inquiry, rather than re-evaluating its relevance.
Just-world hypothesis	The tendency for people to want to believe that the world is fundamentally just, causing them to rationalise an otherwise inexplicable injustice as deserved by the victim(s).	A workplace incident investigator might assume that the injured worker must have been careless or violated safety protocols, believing that incidents only happen to those who behave irresponsibly or unsafely.
Law of the instrument	An over-reliance on a familiar tool or methods, ignoring or under-valuing alternative approaches. "If all you have is a hammer, everything looks like a nail."	A workplace incident investigator might rely heavily on their preferred causation model for all investigations, regardless of its appropriateness or effectiveness.

Name	Description	Example
Look-elsewhere effect	An apparently statistically significant observation may have actually arisen by chance because of the size of the parameter space to be searched.	A workplace incident investigator might focus on easily accessible data, such as worker compliance records or recent safety audits, and find a correlation between poor safety training and the incident. However, by concentrating only on the most readily available data, they may overlook other, less obvious factors—like environmental conditions or faulty equipment—that were equally or more significant contributors to the incident.
Mere exposure effect	The tendency to express undue liking for things merely because of familiarity with them.	A workplace incident investigator might fail to explore potential shortcomings of a particular practice because it's a long-standing practice they see used regularly across many sites, even when evidence of potential shortcomings becomes available.
Naïve realism	The belief that we see reality as it really is – objectively and without bias; that the facts are plain for all to see; that rational people will agree with us; and that those who do not are either uninformed, lazy, irrational, or biased.	A workplace incident investigator might believe that their analysis of the situation is the only logical conclusion, assuming that anyone who disagrees simply lacks understanding or is biased.
Negativity bias or Negativity effect	Psychological phenomenon by which humans have a greater recall of unpleasant memories compared with positive memories.	A workplace incident investigator might give disproportionate weight to a witness due to a challenging interview.

Name	Description	Example
Neglect of probability	The tendency to completely disregard probability when making a decision under uncertainty.	When reviewing an incident involving equipment, a workplace incident investigator might assume that a failure was a rare fluke rather than considering statistical failure rates, maintenance records, and usage patterns that suggest the failure was actually quite probable and preventable.
Normalcy bias	The refusal to plan for, or react to, a disaster which has never happened before.	A workplace incident investigator might assume that the existing safety protocols are adequate because there has not been a serious incident in years. This mindset could lead them to dismiss emerging risks, such as new machinery or changes in work processes, that were not covered by the older protocols.
Not invented here	Aversion to contact with or use of products, research, standards, or knowledge developed outside a group.	An internal workplace incident investigator might dismiss proven safety protocols suggested by external safety experts or other companies, preferring instead to rely on methods developed in-house.
Observer-expectancy effect	When a researcher expects a given result and therefore unconsciously manipulates an experiment or misinterprets data to find it.	A workplace incident investigator expecting to find evidence of poor maintenance practices might unconsciously steer witness interview questions to confirm this belief.
Omission bias	The tendency to judge harmful actions (commissions) as worse, or less moral, than equally harmful inactions (omissions).	A workplace incident investigator might favour inaction over intervention, believing that not performing machine maintenance is less harmful than using a faulty machine.

Name	Description	Example
Outcome bias	The tendency to judge a decision by its eventual outcome instead of based on the quality of the decision at the time it was made.	A workplace incident investigator might conclude that a worker's decision to bypass a safety procedure was reasonable simply because the worker had successfully completed similar tasks without incident in the past.
Overconfidence effect	Excessive confidence in one's own answers to questions. For example, for certain types of questions, answers that people rate as "99% certain" turn out to be wrong 40% of the time.	A workplace incident investigator might overestimate their ability to deduce and weigh causative factors, ignoring the need for additional expertise or consultation.
Parkinson's law of triviality	The tendency to give disproportionate weight to trivial issues. Also known as bike shedding, this bias explains why an organisation may avoid specialised or complex subjects, such as the design of a nuclear reactor, and instead focus on something easy to grasp or rewarding to the average participant, such as the design of an adjacent bike shed.	a workplace incident investigator might focus extensively on small issues, like improper tool storage or minor PPE violations, because they are easy to identify and resolve. Meanwhile, they may neglect deeper, more complex causes of the incident, such as inadequate machinery maintenance or flawed safety protocols, which require more specialised knowledge to address.
Plan continuation bias	Failure to recognise that the original plan of action is no longer appropriate for a changing situation or for a situation that is different than anticipated.	A workplace incident investigator might continue to pursue a line of questioning in a witness interview, despite evidence suggesting a different direction is needed.
Planning fallacy	The tendency to underestimate task-completion times.	A workplace incident investigator might underestimate the time and resources needed to complete a thorough investigation, leading to rushed and incomplete conclusions.

Name	Description	Example
Probative blindness	A phenomenon where organisations fail to update their beliefs about safety, even when they are confronted with mounting evidence to the contrary (see Rae, A.J., Mcdermid, J.A., Alexander, R.D., Nicholson, M. (2014) Probative blindness: how safety activity can fail to update beliefs about safety, in: 9th IET *International Conference on System Safety and Cyber Security* (2014)).	A workplace incident investigator might continue to believe that the company's safety policy of 'zero harm' is effective, despite data suggesting incidents are not being reported. Instead of recommending a policy update based on this evidence, the workplace incident investigator might disregard incidents that were falsely attributed to worker mistakes.
Puritanical bias	Refers to the tendency to attribute cause of an undesirable outcome or wrongdoing by an individual to a moral deficiency or lack of self-control rather than taking into account the impact of broader societal determinants.	A workplace incident investigator might focus on a worker's behaviour as a cause, rather than understanding why a person may have acted in a certain way.
Reactance	The urge to do the opposite of what someone wants you to do out of a need to resist a perceived attempt to constrain your freedom of choice (see also Reverse psychology).	A workplace incident investigator might seek causes other than what has been suggested to them, simply because they perceive them as imposed by others, not based on their own assessment.
Recency illusion	The illusion that a phenomenon one has noticed only recently is itself recent. Often used to refer to linguistic phenomena; the illusion that a word or language usage that one has noticed only recently is an innovation when it is in fact long-established (see also frequency illusion).	A workplace incident investigator might start seeing more cases of fatigue-related incidents and stress claims, they might assume that worker mental health issues have only recently become a problem. In fact, workplace stress and fatigue have always been present but may not have been openly discussed or recognised in past investigations.

Name	Description	Example
Restraint bias	The tendency to overestimate one's ability to show restraint in the face of temptation.	A workplace incident investigator might overestimate their ability to resist biases and remain objective, leading to unrecognised personal biases influencing the investigation.
Risk compensation / Peltzman effect	The tendency to take greater risks when perceived safety increases.	A workplace incident investigator might use a familiar and popular investigation model and methodology, despite that model and methodology not being well-suited to the nature of the incident.
Salience bias	The tendency to focus on items that are more prominent or emotionally striking and ignore those that are unremarkable, even though this difference is often irrelevant by objective standards.	A workplace incident investigator might focus on more dramatic and noticeable causes, like visible machinery malfunctions, while ignoring less obvious but equally dangerous risks, like exposure to repetitive strain injuries.
Selection bias	The tendency to notice or give more weight to something when we become more aware of it, such as noticing cars similar to our own after purchasing one. Also known as Observational Selection Bias.	A workplace incident investigator might base their conclusions on a non-representative sample of incidents. For example, they might focus solely on hazards reported in one department, not considering that this department may simply be the only one actively reporting hazards, leading to an incomplete understanding of overall safety issues.
Selective perception	The tendency for expectations to affect perception.	A workplace incident investigator might only notice safety issues that confirm their pre-existing beliefs, ignoring evidence that contradicts them.

Name	Description	Example
Semmelweis reflex	The tendency to reject new evidence that contradicts a paradigm.	A workplace incident investigator might dismiss evidence suggesting that workplace stress and fatigue significantly contribute to incidents because the prevailing belief within the organisation is that most incidents are caused by individual worker mistakes rather than systemic factors.
Shared information bias	Known as the tendency for group members to spend more time and energy discussing information that all members are already familiar with (i.e., shared information), and less time and energy discussing information that only some members are aware of (i.e., unshared information).	During an Incident Investigation Analysis Team meeting, team members might focus primarily on known safety risks and previously identified hazards rather than exploring new or less obvious contributing factors. As a result, unique insights from individuals with different experiences or roles may be overlooked.
Stereotyping	Expecting a member of a group to have certain characteristics without having actual information about that individual.	A workplace incident investigator might assume that younger employees are more prone to incidents, leading to biased scrutiny and potentially unfair blame, despite a lack of evidence for this.
Subadditivity effect	The tendency to judge probability of the whole to be less than the probabilities of the parts.	A workplace incident investigator might underestimate the cumulative effect of incident causes by evaluating its components separately rather than considering the combined effect.
Subjective validation	Perception that something is true if a subject's belief demands it to be true. Also assigns perceived connections between coincidences.	A workplace incident investigator might give undue weight to personal experiences or anecdotal evidence that supports their hypotheses, ignoring contradictory data.

Name	Description	Example
Survivorship bias	Concentrating on the people or things that "survived" some process and inadvertently overlooking those that did not because of their lack of visibility.	A workplace incident investigator might focus on successful safety practices that have worked in the past, ignoring those that failed and were discontinued. This can result in an incomplete understanding of what actually works.
System justification	The tendency to defend and bolster the status quo. Existing social, economic, and political arrangements tend to be preferred, and alternatives disparaged, sometimes even at the expense of individual and collective self-interest. (See also status quo bias.)	A workplace incident investigator might resist recommending new, more radical changes believing that the current system is fundamentally sound despite increasing evidence of frequent incidents.
Systematic Bias	A tendency for the established systems, processes, or structures within an organisation to consistently produce unfair or skewed outcomes. This bias is not due to individual prejudice but arises from the way the system operates, affecting judgements and decisions across the board.	The structure of the organisation may discourage lower-level employees from speaking openly about safety concerns due to fear of retaliation or a lack of trust in the reporting process. If an investigator primarily gathers input from management or safety professionals, they may miss critical frontline perspectives on the root causes of safety issues.
Trait ascription bias	The tendency for people to view themselves as relatively variable in terms of personality, behaviour, and mood while viewing others as much more predictable.	A workplace incident investigator might assume that workers consistently follow safe behaviours. This assumption overlooks the reality that individuals may behave differently due to a range of factors, such as personal circumstances, environmental pressures, or differing interpretations of safety protocols.

Name	Description	Example
Ultimate attribution error	Similar to the fundamental attribution error, in this error a person is likely to make an internal attribution to an entire group instead of the individuals within the group.	A workplace incident investigator might believe that incidents involving workers from a particular demographic (e.g., temporary workers) are due to inherent, internal deficiencies within that group, such as lack of skill or commitment, while attributing incidents involving permanent employees to external factors like poor equipment or hazardous conditions.

Acknowledgements

I am deeply grateful to my wife and family for their enduring love and encouragement throughout this journey.

Thank you to Andrew Evans, Jared Kane, and Gregory Smith for your encouragement, insights, and generous support. Your feedback and professional influence helped shape this book into something practical, focused, and hopefully useful to the people doing the work.

"An interesting and helpful piece of work. The book offers clear, structured guidance for incident investigations that, if well applied, should result in more coherent and comprehensible outcomes. It adds real value to the field by encouraging clarity of thought regardless of investigation methodology."

— Greg Smith, WHS Lawyer & Author, Paper Safe

About the Author

Desai Link is a work health and safety professional who has worked across Australia and New Zealand. His experience spans industries including construction, infrastructure, transport, oil and gas, and hospitality. Desai has led a wide range of health and safety investigations involving physical and psychological harm and is known for his practical, ethical approach to getting to the heart of what happened—and what needs to happen next.

He is admitted as a lawyer to the Supreme Court of Western Australia and lectures on health and safety law and investigations at Auckland University of Technology. Desai regularly speaks at professional forums, conferences, and webinars, and is co-host of the Circus of Safety podcast.

Beyond the Incident is his first book.

If You Found This Book Helpful

If Beyond the Incident gave you clarity, confidence, or a new way of thinking about investigations, the most helpful thing you can do is leave a short review on Amazon. Even a sentence or a star rating helps other practitioners find the book and benefit from it.

Thank you for supporting honest, practical safety work.

For further information, speaking inquiries, or training resources, please contact me on LinkedIn.

www.ingramcontent.com/pod-product-compliance
Lightning Source LLC
Chambersburg PA
CBHW032137020426
42334CB00016B/1196